THE END OF ALL OUR EXPLORING

Developing a Friendship with God

> We shall not cease from exploration
> And the end of all our exploring
> Will be to arrive where we started
> And know the place for the first time.
>
> T.S. Eliot, 'Little Gidding'

DR. KELLY JAMES BONEWELL

Sed nobis Press

Scriptures taken from the Holy Bible, New International Version®, NIV®. Copyright © 1973, 1978, 1984, 2011 by Biblica, Inc.™ Used by permission of Zondervan. All rights reserved worldwide.
www.zondervan.com The "NIV" and "New International Version" are trademarks registered in the United States Patent and Trademark Office by Biblica, Inc.™

THE END OF ALL OUR EXPLORING: DEVELOPING A FRIENDSHIP WITH GOD. Copyright © 2011 by Kelly James Bonewell. All rights reserved. No part of this publication may be reproduced, stored in a retrieval system, or transmitted in any form or by any means— electronic, mechanical, photocopy, recording or any other— except for brief quotations in printed reviews, without the prior permission of the author.

Library of Congress Cataloging - in-Publication Data

Cover design: Anthony Brugada

Cover painting: Caravaggio, Supper at Emmaus, 1601. Photo by Allison DeGrauve.

Bonewell, Kelly
    The end of all our exploring : developing a friendship with God / Kelly Bonewell — 1st ed.
       p. cm.

    Includes bibliographical references.
    ISBN13-978-0615940816 (Sednobis Press)
    ISBN-10-0615940811
 1. Trust in God—Christianity.   2. Christian Life.   I. Title.

Printed in the United States of America

This book is dedicated to
Julie Beth Bonewell
Josiah William Bonewell,
and Micah James Bonewell.

So glad we share this life together.

CONTENTS

Part One: The Underpinnings of Faith
8

Part Two: Just Believing in God
54

Part Three: Following Too Hard After God
94

Part Four: Moving into Friendship with God
167

Epilogue: Learning to Walk on the Water
246

Part One
The Underpinnings of Faith

HOW LOOKING AT A CARAVAGGIO PAINTING CAN CHANGE YOUR LIFE

A painter should begin every canvas with a wash of black, because all things in nature are dark except where exposed by the light.

Leonardo da Vinci

I have read in Plato and Cicero sayings that are wise and very beautiful; but I have never read in either of them: Come unto me all ye that labor and are heavy laden.

St. Augustine

Almost twenty-five years ago, shortly after becoming a Christian, I came across a remarkable painting. I was at my school's library in downtown Chicago—Grant Park was right outside the window from where I sat. As I turned the page of a book the 15th century Italian painter Michelangelo Caravaggio's *The Supper at Emmaus* caught my eye. I was flipping through a bunch of books that I had grabbed off the shelves. I was just wasting time, waiting for a class to begin. Immediately, this painting caught my eye, because it wasn't your typical "religious" artwork. In fact, it was almost too non-descript, and at first I didn't realize that it was a painting depicting anything sacred or religious—it just looked like a painting of a few guys eating lunch together. I've only seen this painting in art books, and one day, I hope to venture to the National Gallery in London and see it up close.

That day when I caught sight of this painting, it began for me a new way of seeing Jesus. Something was special about this painting, made up of nothing more than oils placed with some thought and skill on the canvas. As I sat and stared at it, I realized why it held my attention and I recognized its uniqueness. It was how the characters looked. When I open up an art book now and flip to the painting, I realize that it depicts the friendship of God in an astonishing manner. Back then, you know what caught my eye? Simply this, Jesus looks real. Gone is the blond hair and blue eyes. He looks like a real Hebrew guy, olive skin and all. Caravaggio did something earth shattering in his time as an artist—he painted Jesus like a real person; amazingly, he looked human and real to life. In fact, very uncommon for his time, most of Caravaggio's models were peasants from local villages. Instead of painting the noble and the wealthy as his models for John the Baptist, Jesus or any other biblical character, he was painting the cobblers, fishermen and maidens of his day, and therefore, when it came to religious art, for the first time ever, his paintings took on a look that was authentic and true.

In this painting of Caravaggio's, Jesus looks like a person; someone you could know, the guy next door. He seems approachable. This is the operative word—Jesus in this painting looks like a *person*. Before this, in the art world—for the artist, Jesus was never a person—He was just "God." Most of the artists in this period were painting the "majestic Christ"—the unapproachable Jesus, the one on the throne, the one you needed to schedule by appointment. But none of this actually captured the biblical narrative, because as we know, Jesus really is a person, a friend, and someone who is very approachable. With Caravaggio's interpretation, you see this "friend" aspect come out onto the canvas. Jesus is just hanging out, eating a meal and shootin' the breeze. When I saw this painting, this was in my early years of being a Christian and this was the Jesus I wanted to get to know. You could get close to him and this was what I wanted. Unlike other religious art I had seen up to that point, it captured Jesus as someone you would want to get to know. As a contrast, go look at some of the art work from this period or earlier and you will notice that the characterizations of Jesus are oblong and uncomfortable. Let me illustrate some examples; you might have seen some paintings depicting Jesus like this:

- Painting No. 1: Baby Jesus is pure white and his face looks like

he's 59 years old—wrinkled and balding. He wears a smirk, a baptismal gown and a bratty look.
- Painting No. 2: Jesus has his kingly pose, no smile, wearied look and it looks as if he might want to think about getting a prescription for some Prozac.

Again, these portrayals of Jesus' just aren't realistic. They don't tell the real story that the Bible tells. These works of art do not depict Jesus as he really is. However, Caravaggio was getting into it, painting as if he was there, sitting at the very table, and showing you something sacred and important. Again, this is the Jesus we are going to try to encounter in this book. The real one.

WE EACH HAVE TWO POCKETS

It is not what you say that matters but the manner in which you say it; there lies the secret of the ages.

William Carlos Williams

Everyone must have two pockets, so that he can reach into the one or the other, according to his needs. In his right pocket are to be the words: "For my sake the world was created," and in his left: "I am dust and ashes."

Martin Buber

Did you know that in the Bible, there is a quote from a Greek pagan poet? Paul in the book of Acts cites the poet Aratus (271-213 BC) from his book of poetry *Phaenomena* to make a point about God. Aratus penned the words that we find in Acts 17:28, "For in him we live and move and have our being." Paul slyly used these words to drive home the argument to his Greek listeners that God could be found and not in something fashioned out of gold or silver. Aratus had something to say and it was profound, even though he perhaps didn't fully realize the implications as he wrote those words almost three hundred years earlier. Aratus is not a well-known poet today, and yet, the Bible has made his words literally eternal! God has sometimes used the pagan or non-Christian to murmur the profound. God can use anyone at any time to offer his truth, even when they might not even know it.

Martin Buber, a Jewish theologian, wrote something insightful and important which is quoted at the beginning of this chapter. These words above are profound and central to this book. In my work as a pastor and counselor, I have the tremendous privilege of hearing the secrets of people's lives. You should hear the stuff I get to hear—wives unloading dark pasts that have never been uttered; young men in tears struggling deeply with their futures and desires; couples speaking in stark honesty about the grueling disconnectedness of their love for one another. Because of the ethic of confidentiality that is inherent in caring for these people, these individuals finally feel they have the freedom to unburden their lives and I sometimes am the auspicious recipient to their private thoughts.

What Buber talks about in this quotation is exactly where I find people struggling the most. They perhaps know in their minds that "for the sake of the world they were created," but it has yet to seep down practically in their lives and because of this, words such as these are distant to them. Think about that phrase for a minute—*for the sake of the world you were created*—that is a truth that the Bible time and time again tries to explain to us.

However, Buber in this quote, only got it part right. If we are to be entirely correct and biblical, we would need to add to his words—"for the sake of being in relationship with God, you were created." The Creator of the universe, THE I AM, Elohim, Yahweh, Jesus also created you to be in relationship with him. He deeply desires to be close to you. This is first and foremost, God created you for one purpose, because he wanted to have a relationship with you. Just as much as he desired for you to have a relationship with him; he equally desires to have a relationship with you. This was the whole of creation, the purpose of the creation story—the story boiled down to its core—it is that God desired to be in a relationship with us. Granted, many of us know about this. We heard it in Sunday school or from some pastor one Sunday morning, but this is the point—we may know about it, but we might not know it for ourselves, and experience this truth down into our bones. We can maybe sing the words *Jesus, loves me, this I know*, but the words are voiced, but not truly believed.

Most I meet who are struggling, know Buber's concluding words the best—"I am dust and ashes." Too many people that I meet, especially those who call themselves Christians, know very little in terms of experience of who they were created to be. They base their worth on something else rather than their relationship with God. They base it on their work, or on a relationship, or on a tradition, or something oddly different. This is where a lot of my work as a pastor and therapist tends to lean—getting individuals to see who they are in Jesus' eyes. The human person in their fallen state has such black and white thinking. We are either great or we are either nothing. We either think too highly of ourselves or too little. There is usually no middle ground with us; and in many cases, and for some of us, we tend to move toward seeing ourselves too poorly. As one example, the medieval theologian John Calvin wrote some important and good things, but teaching that we are "but a rottenness and a worm" (Calvin 39) was not one of them. How often I see people gravitate toward this type of thinking about themselves and the ramifications are terribly damaging. There is balance in the Christian life and too often we lean too much in one direction or the other. The Bible is clear—while it is true that we are sinners, we can also be saints.

THE DIFFICULT QUESTION EACH OF US MUST ASK

The outward work will never be puny if the inward work is great. And the outward work can never be great or even good if the inward one is puny or of little worth. The inward work invariably includes in itself all expansiveness, all breadth, all length, all depth. Such a work receives and draws all its being from nowhere else except from and in the heart of God. Meister Eckhart

Some people feel the rain. Others just get wet. Bob Dylan

The other night I was watching a show on television and a woman being interviewed said that she had grown up in a "good Christian" home. I've heard that phrase a lot lately. We all want to be good Christians, don't we? But the question is—what is a "good Christian?" Is a good Christian one who says they believe in God? Is a good Christian one who does all the right things: doesn't go see rated R movies, or cuss, spit or have tattoos? Is a good Christian one who goes to church every Sunday and every Wednesday? Is a good Christian one who reads the Bible every morning without missing a single day for years and years? Is a good Christian one who serves down at the homeless shelter every other weekend? Is a good Christian one who prays before each meal, head bowed and eyes closed? Is a good Christian one who has memorized a whole slew of Bible verses and can recite them on command? Is a good Christian someone who tithes 15% of their gross income? Is a good Christian one who commits his life to being a pastor, a deacon or a missionary to some forgotten world? What exactly is a good Christian? I think a good Christian is one who loves God with all their heart, mind, soul, and strength and then also loves their neighbor as themselves. But one can only do that by being in an ever-growing relationship with Jesus. These are Jesus' words—not mine.

So with this, some years ago I was asked one of the most difficult questions I have ever encountered as a therapist. The question caught me off guard. A young wife stared at me seriously and almost in a whisper, reluctantly asked a simple, but profound question. Her words were uncomplicated as she asked, "How do I have a relationship with God?" You have to understand that this was a twenty-six year old woman who had grown up in the church, had attended church for many years, and I know for a fact, heard some very good sermons on this very question while attending there. Yet this question kept at her, so much so that in the silence that sometimes disturbs a counseling session, her question emerged, and it probably lingered in her for years unspoken. However, her problem was not so straightforward. She was really asking a more complex question—*how do I know God?* I thought—now, that is a question! It made me wonder, how many others also wish to ask that very question?

Beyond this, she was looking for something that she had never experienced—she did her devotions; she attended church regularly; she stood up and sang the songs during the worship during the service. This young woman was looking for friendship. As Bernard of Clairvaux said nearly a thousand years ago about his relationship with God, "I have a friend. I have freed my soul." Think about that—what does that mean to have your soul freed? That's what this client of mine wanted; she wanted to be freed. Yet she knew deep in her heart the relationship with God she had was not doing this—there was little, if any, freedom in her soul. She knew deep down that there was something more dynamic, more all-encompassing and she wanted it.

Very slowly, I began to explain to her this process and the journey I will detail in this book. To be honest, I had to think about that question more deeply than I ever had. I wanted to give her the right answer and not just a line. This is where this book comes from—one Thursday evening a young wife asked a question that called out to be answered—

how can someone have a freeing relationship with their Creator? Brennan Manning paints the answer to this question in bright colors: "Religion is not a matter of learning how to think about God, but actually encountering him." This woman, like so many others, no longer wanted to just think about God or play games with him, she desired to encounter him. Was that even possible?

THE NECESSITY TO GROW

Everything you want in life is right outside your comfort zone. Robert Allen
God draws, but He draws the willing one. John Chrysostom

As I thought about this woman that I mentioned in the previous section, it dawned on me just how imperative it is to continually pursue God. As an example of this, I know of someone who recently has walked away from their faith. This was a person who some years back was serving and living a life that was exemplary when it came to being a Christian. However, over the last couple of years, I began to see that this life began to wane and he did not take his relationship with God very seriously over these last years. Slowly over time, it began to show, and not only with the obvious outward signs. Sadly, since that time, he has made many poor decisions, which has not only impacted him negatively, but his family as well. It's been a little bit like watching a train wreck.

Of late, I have been thinking about how unhealthy it can be to not have Jesus at the center of your life on a daily basis. Yet this happens all the time. In general, the church today places such emphasis on evangelism, "getting people saved and into heaven," but focuses too little on discipleship—learning how to live a life with Jesus. The Barna Group has some staggering statistics, confirming the fact that the church is good at "making converts, but not disciples:"

- In a recent study, when Christian adults were asked to identify their most important goal for their life, not a single person said it was to be a committed follower of Jesus Christ.
- Less than one out of every five born again adults had any specific and measurable goals related to their personal spiritual development.
- Less than 1% of all Christians perceived a connection between

- their efforts to worship God and their development as a disciple of Jesus.
- The most widely-known Bible verse among adult and teen Christians is "God helps those who help themselves"—which is not actually in the Bible, and conflicts with the basic message of Scripture.

Living with Jesus every day—this is really where life begins, not when you say the sinner's prayer. Life is always continuing and we need to move with it. However, too often in Christian circles, being reflective and deliberate about our relationship with God is put to the side. For whatever reason, people tend to stagnate rather than thrive after making a commitment of faith. Questions don't get asked. Masks begin to be worn. We play the part, but in reality, we don't know how to genuinely be in friendship with God. Living the Christian life and going through the motions is easy, being in relationship with Jesus is a whole different matter. This is what he was talking about when he told the parable about building your life on the sand—that it was unsafe to build on something that is temporary.

After becoming a Christian, I learned an important lesson—if you have any amount of biblical knowledge, watch out. You eventually will become the expert, the guru. People will perceive that you have it all together, look up to you, and believe that you and God must be best buds. But all of this can be dangerous, because it can perpetuate a serious problem—you will begin to learn how to live an inauthentic life; you learn how to fake it. In the end, you will paint yourself into a corner to which there is no escape. Because you have played the role of the well-behaved churchgoer, you won't know how to play any other part. Sadly, I know this from first-hand experience from years past.

But religious knowledge is never the standard for having a relationship with God and too often in the church, this is what we emphasize. It's easy to know a lot about someone; it's a whole new thing to know someone. This makes sense—it's much more easy and comfortable to just know about someone, simply knowing the facts (e.g., "she works at a hospital, likes to eat salads at lunch, has three kids, and drives a white Toyota Sienna."). There's distance and safety and very little mess. But knowing just the facts about someone does not mean you know them. Lots of us know a lot of stuff about a whole bunch of people, but it goes about as far as that. Our knowledge is a mile wide, but an inch deep. For some, it can be rare that we have genuinely deep and strong friendships. We keep people at bay, at a safe distance and we don't go too deep. We can also do the same with God.

But we need to move beyond just knowing about God—we need to push to know him personally. John Wesley once wrote, "Once in seven years I burn all my sermons; for it is a shame, if I cannot write better sermons now than I did seven years ago." In that statement, Wesley was saying that it was not a good thing if he hadn't grown beyond where he once stood in terms of knowing God. We need to keep moving on as well, being restless and asking for more. This should be our end goal. I think C.S. Lewis said it in the most direct way possible:

> Every time you make a choice, you are turning the central part of you, the part of you that chooses, into something a little different from what it was before. And, taking your life as a whole, with all your innumerable choices, all your life long you are slowly turning this central thing either into a Heaven creature or into a hellish creature—either into a creature that is in harmony with God, and with other creatures, and with itself, or else into one that is in a state of war and hatred with God, and with its fellow creatures and with itself.

Those are strong and difficult words, but they are true. Yogi Berra said it in a similar way, but in a way only he could: "If you don't know where you're going, you'll end up somewhere else." As Christians, we need to continually change and grow and move beyond just knowing about God and genuinely encounter him. At the end of the day, we need to know where we are headed.

A VERY SIMPLE THEOLOGICAL PRIMER

Do you wish to be great? Then begin by being. Do you desire to construct a vast and lofty fabric? Think first about the foundations of humility. The higher your structure is to be, the deeper must be its foundation.

St Augustine

The Kingdom of Heaven is not for the well-meaning: it is for the desperate.

James Denney

But let's go back to that fundamental question—how does one come into a relationship with God, the Creator of the universe, the One who is beyond beyond? What are the steps we need to make to know him? How do you enter into a relationship with the One who made the stars that make up the Big Dipper, the power and magnificence of the Atlantic Ocean, you and me. When one thinks about it in those terms, on paper, it seems impossible. Me? A relationship with God? Why would he ever want that? How can that ever happen?

Sometimes, a necessary step in moving deeper into a relationship with God is changing how we view him. At this point, we should discuss a little theology. With my work as a counselor and pastor, sometimes my work is guiding someone in making a modification in their life—for example, a slight alteration in thinking can bring on a whole different outlook. How we view ourselves and God can entirely alter the direction of our lives. Put more plainly, sometimes we need to revise how we think about God and who he is.

Let me offer an example of what I mean by this. I love to play golf. It is a game that captures many difficult and trying aspects: concentration, finesse, power and agility. There are many reasons why I enjoy hitting that little white ball. For one, it allows me to be outdoors and see the beauty of creation. Even though Mark Twain commented that it was "a good walk spoiled," I don't mind that. Even if I am hitting the ball every which way, and not in the direction I want it to go—on an August evening out on a golf course is what I imagine to be a little bit of heaven. It is also a game in which consistency is a key element if one wants to improve. With golf, a rhythm needs to occur to play well and sometimes how you swing the club can have the slightest miscue, which can lead to a terrible shot. A small alteration—the position of your stance, how you grip the club or how you pull back the club—can make all the difference in hitting a shot onto the fairway or one that is deep into the trees where the poison ivy grows. When you spend lots of time at the golf range, in working on these changes, you can begin to hit the ball where you want. It takes practice, but when you hit that one shot which lands on the green and fairly close to the cup, this is what keeps you coming back for more. But for this to happen, it often takes one small, but important change in what you are currently doing wrong.

For some, this is a parallel of what needs to happen to us as it pertains to our view of God. Sometimes, we just need to re-adjust how we view God—not make dramatic changes, just make minor shifts. Some of the people I work with in counseling or who I have met with as a pastor have disjointed views about God and this creates all types of havoc in their lives. Sometimes, it is not on the surface, but lurking underneath. As we slowly get at the root, they can begin to see how their view of God is not biblical or right. Overtime, such thinking has warped their idea about God, but also about themselves and others. This is a truth—when you have a false view of God, everything can be false thereafter. Here are a few examples:
- "No, God is nothing like your dad who always told you how you would never amount to anything."
- "No, God is not out to get you."
- "No, God isn't like the slot machines in Vegas."

This is always the first stride in living right, lining up our view of God with what is true and accurate. Essentially, it is a modern parallel of destroying our idols, because this is exactly what idolatry is—a false idea about God. Here are just a few essential truths about God:

- He is good and kind.
- He doesn't only love you, he likes you.
- He is on your side.
- He desires to do a tremendous thing in your life.

But those above phrases are too easy, aren't they? If we grew up in the church, we learn these things in kindergarten. Usually, they don't stick then, and they don't stick now. Platitudes are easy to say, but very difficult to experience. How can we get these ideas to sink in and not be just words that we say? This is the first step in aligning our theology in terms of having correct ideas about who God is and, just as importantly, what we mean to him.

TAKING ANOTHER LOOK AT WHO WE ARE

And this takes us to another important and vital step—it is to begin to change how we see ourselves. The book of Romans calls this "a renewing of the mind" (Romans 12:2). This requires that we change how we look at God, but also how we view ourselves and why we were created in the first place. In this second step toward a more sound theology, one needs to take a step back and look at the tale of redemption as a whole, and see how they fit into that story. An essential part of the process is coming to know who you are as a person in God's eyes. However, many people have a hard time here. A common process is: (1) our theology or ideas about God become skewed, and (2) then our conception about ourselves gets off kilter as well. Here is an example of this—each of us has to answer an important question—why did God create you in the first place? To answer this, here is another key theological premise: *You are made in the image of God; you are God's child.*

Mediate on that statement for a minute. Go for a short walk and think about the ramifications of that statement—you are God's child;

you were made in the image of God. Just twenty six sentences into the book God wrote, he declares this magnificent truth, "Let us make human beings in our image, in our likeness." (Genesis 1:26) That is an amazing statement. This is something to take in and really think about. However, too often we ramble over that amazing assertion, and yet that is the starting point of the entire Scriptures, the entire story of the Bible. The central part of the story of Scriptures is the story of a very special creation—specifically, God's children. As an illustration, in any story or novel that you could read, be it *The Christmas Carol* or *The Adventures of Huckleberry Finn,* there are central characters to the story; in this one, the two main characters of the Bible are God, and the sparkle of his eye, his children. That is the crux of the biblical story. Read the Bible in its entirety and you will see that theme found in its story over and over. In a unique way, at the end of the day, the story found in the Bible is about you and the Almighty.

Let's look at one final essential about you and I found in the Bible. The ancient father of the early church, Athanasius (d. 373) boldly asserted that "God became man so that men might become gods." Doesn't that sound seriously blasphemous? Can you imagine your pastor using that quote for a sermon some Sunday morning? There's one problem with this—this guy Athanasius is one of the pillars in constructing Christian theology and doctrine in the early church. A lot of his writings are regarded on the same plane as St. Augustine or any other ancient Christian philosopher (on a side note, C.S. Lewis thought very highly of Athanasius and called his book *De Incarnatione,* a "masterpiece"). In other words, this guy wasn't some cultic whacko writing these words; he was a conservative theologian who the church looked to for doctrinal guidance.

But what was he attempting to say with that statement—that God became man so that men might become gods? As I read those words, it tilts toward another notion about us as a people and creation. The point would be this: *We, as human beings, as God's children, have been given redemption; our lives have literally been rescued and redeemed because we are a unique creation unlike anything God has created and his desire is that we become like him.*

But what does that mean? Looking forward to Jesus, the truth is that his sacrifice on the cross was for us as human beings, but here is a crucial point, we are not the only "characters" in this story that the Bible tells. In particular, you have intertwined in this story that God has also created another special being, a very unique creation as well. As we all know, the Bible calls these creations angels (Job 38:4-7; Daniel 7:10; Nehemiah 9:6; Psalm 148:2,5; Hebrews 1:14). Strangely, in terms of redemption, Jesus does not sacrifice his life for these beings on the cross (Job 1:6, Galatians 4:5-6, 1 Peter: 1:12, Hebrews 2:5). Why is this? They "fell" too, didn't they? Just like us, they disobeyed God, didn't they? When we move forward in the story and learn about Jesus and his crucifixion, why is his death not redemptive for these that God created as well?

This then becomes a very important point in terms of our story as a creation. The question then becomes—what makes us so special? Why are we saved and the fallen angels are not? Why are they not given an opportunity to repent and turn back to God? To answer this question, we have to go back to Athanasius and his idea that "God became man so that men might become gods." To begin, you have to read Psalm 8:5-6 from the World English Bible; it is one of the few translations in English that translates these verses correctly from the original Hebrew:

> What is man, that you think of him? The son of man, that you care for him? For you have made him a little lower than God, And crowned him with glory and honor. You make him ruler over the works of your hands. You have put all things under his feet.

Most English translations such as the New International Version or King James Version interpret this verse differently and they alter that one phrase to say that we were made a little lower than the angels. The problem is that the word used in that verse is the Hebrew word *Elohim*, which of course, we know is the most used name for God in the Old Testament (used a measly 3,500 times). Back in the 14th century, perhaps when John Wycliffe and others were translating the Scriptures into English from the Greek and Latin, they just could not write out such a bold claim. *Just below God? We are made a little lower than God?* No, these writers must have thought, what the Psalmist must have meant in that verse is that the human creation was made subject to heavenly and angelic beings—we were made lower than them. Yet how wrong they were. In fact, that verse translated in that way is actually un-biblical. Again, going back to the book of Genesis, you were made in the image of the living God; He gave himself up for you, because this is how much you are worth as his child. You are priceless. This is how uniquely extraordinary you are and this is what makes Jesus' sacrifice for us so important and so unmatched. Can you see how important you are in the grand scheme of creation? Can you begin to see how important you are to God?

THE JEALOUS FOE

Be who God meant you to be and you will set the world on fire.
St. Catherine of Siena

Our duty, as men and women, is to proceed as if limits to our ability did not exist. We are collaborators in creation.
Teilhard de Chardin

There are two equal and opposite errors into which our race can fall about devils. One is to disbelieve in their existence. The other is to believe, and to feel an excessive and unhealthy interest in them.
C.S. Lewis

But this is not the full story. Let's listen to another part of the story that God wants to share. We need to go way back; back to the beginning, even before we were created. An important character of the Bible shows up who also is very crucial to its story. In fact, he is the antagonist, our opponent, enemy and foe. He is the nemesis, and he is a formidable one (not to God, but to his children and to his creation). His name is Lucifer (or Satan) and he is an essential character in the story of God's purposes of creation and redemption and it can be a great danger to forget that.

To begin, Lucifer was and is a very unique being. In terms of understanding who this person is, in the book of Ezekiel, we are painted a portrait of who this remarkable angelic being was before his rebellion and fall.

> You were in Eden, the garden of God; every precious stone adorned you: ruby, topaz, emerald, chrysolite, onx, jasper, sapphire, turquoise, and beryl. Gold work of tambourines and of pipes was in you. In the day that you were created they were prepared. You were the anointed cherub who covers: and I set you, so that you were on the

holy mountain of God; you have walked up and down in the midst of the stones of fire. You were perfect in your ways from the day that you were created, until unrighteousness was found in you. (Ezekiel 28: 13-15)

The Message translates one section of these verses, this way: "A robe was prepared for you the same day you were created." In this telling, we can think of the story of Joseph and the favoritism from his father Isaac when he was given his special coat of many colors (Genesis 37: 3-4). With a passage like that, it is obvious that Lucifer is favored by God as well. But this is where significant problems begin to emerge in the story —God had other plans.

God earlier was partial to Lucifer, but now he has decided to create someone even more favored, even more beautiful, and I dare say, with even more authority than this beautiful prince. Lucifer (see Isaiah 14:12-15) was one awesome creature, but now he was about to be subject to another creation and people. Simply put—we, as human beings supplanted Lucifer as God's beloved. In terms of the overall plan, we were the rightful heirs right from the beginning. In reading the Scriptures, it can be surmised that Lucifer's jealousy of man began a whirlwind of destruction that we are still subject to today. Again, understanding who we are in the story is of utmost importance. To help spell this out better, below is the hierarchy of the creation in terms of the position of God, the angelic beings, and mankind as his creation.

Before Creation
- God
- Lucifer and the angels

After Creation
- God
- Human creation
- Lucifer (Satan), the fallen angels and angels

After the Fall of Man

- God
- Lucifer (Satan), the fallen angels and angels
- Human creation

After the Death and Resurrection of Jesus Christ

- God
- Human creation
- Lucifer (Satan), the fallen angels and angels

Specifically, if we reframe this understanding of the "hierarchy" of God's creation, it begins to paint with broad strokes where Lucifer fits into the center of this story. If we, being made in God's image, can now begin to understand why this fallen and evil creature wanted our destruction, we can begin to understand why we are so important and why our lives are so crucial to the makeup of this world.

The delineation above tells us some important theological insights. First, after God created the earth and Adam and Eve, human beings not only had dominion over the earth, but over Lucifer and the angels as well. However, here's the bad news and a very important, but tragic point: after man disobeyed God, Lucifer now has now taken dominion and authority over God's treasured creation, his children. In essence, when we Adam and Eve "obeyed" Lucifer, when they followed him into his lie, when they disregarded God's command for their lives—on paper, it was all over and lost. The New Testament spells out what Genesis tries to tell us:

> As for you, you were dead in your transgressions and sins, in which you used to live when you followed the ways of this world and of the ruler of the kingdom of the air, the spirit who is now at work in those who are disobedient (Ephesians 2:2).

In the early part of the book of Genesis, we see this example when it tells the story of the Fall. As we go on and flip a page or two into the book of Genesis, the passage describes this awful situation with greater clarity. In this jealousy Lucifer had toward God's children, in his great hatred toward us, he attempts to lead us away from the One who truly loves us—and with nothing more than a piece of fruit, with just a simple red apple that you could pick on a cold October day.

> The Serpent: "Did God really say, 'You must not eat from any tree in the garden?'"
>
> The Woman: "...God did say 'You must not eat fruit from the tree that is in the middle of the garden, and you must not touch it, or you will die.'"
>
> The Serpent: "You will not surely die..."

Before night fell, Lucifer succeeded in his manipulation and lie, and God's children found themselves subject to a different ruler—to this evil and fallen being. In the Fall, in our disobedience to God, we obeyed our enemy and became his slave. This can be missed when reading Genesis. This is the aspect of reading the Bible as a narrative and not only looking for the obvious. At this point in time, the entire world is under the dominion of this rebellious angel. As we have said, the Bible calls him Lucifer (or Satan in the New Testament) and in different passages he is called "the god of this age" (2 Corinthians 4:4), "the prince of this world" (John 12:31), and "the prince of the power of the air" (Ephesians 2:2). As Milton writes in Paradise Lost, "Satan exalted sat, by merit raised to that bad eminence." That day the world turned sour or as Sally Mann has said, "The earth [became] sculpted out of death." Because Lucifer knew his demise, what a better way to end it—to destroy the creation God loved and treasured the most.

YOU GOTTA SERVE SOMEBODY

Let's talk a little bit more about theology. A new thing happens and

God does not forget about his cherished ones. As Jesus, he comes onto the scene and restores what had become so messed up—not only is he our substitute, but he also ransoms us from Satan's hand. What does that mean? For some of us, when we think about the cross, we immediately think of the phrase—Jesus died for our sins—theologically, this premise is what we call substitutionary atonement. However, in the early church, they viewed the cross in another way; they saw Jesus' death as a ransom for our lives, as a deliverance and protection from Satan's authority over mankind. After the Fall, the human race literally became his property and possession. Theologians from the early church up until the present call this ransom atonement. After the death and resurrection of Jesus, all that is nullified—Satan's reign and control can be over if you want it to be.

So often when Jesus spoke to people he asked them to follow him and this was the reason—to follow him meant that we would literally be turning our back on the one who hates us and we could begin to learn how to live with the One who always had our best at heart. If we were to follow Jesus, everything could be as it should be—we now have restored to us the privilege of being an heir and child of God, and we no longer have to be subject to someone who does not care for us in the least. We now literally give our lives back to God and release ourselves from Satan's control and contempt (to learn more about this premise, you can google Christus Victor). As a central teaching of the New Testament about Jesus' death on the cross, it contends that God not only saves us from sin and death, but also Satan's hatred and control.

Let's look at this concept from one more angle. I love literature. I studied it in college and it is still one of my favorite things to do—to read stories. I have learned so much through them. Drama, tragedy, comedy—they illustrate for us in exceptional ways important truths about life. Stories teach us the most. This is why Jesus spent so much time telling them—it is how we learn best. They stick with us and this is why Jesus spoke truths through parables and stories. The problem is that stories don't always spell it out. You have to read them (and sometimes reread) and listen for what they are trying to say. Sometimes, it's not so obvious to understand what the author is trying to say. And when you think about it, the Bible is written almost exclusively as a story when one reads it cover to cover. Sometimes when we read the Scriptures, we need to remember to read it that way—simply as we would read an exhilarating novel that a friend has recommended. Walter Wangerin did us a great service when he wrote *The Book of God*, because it brought us back to the fundamentals of the story of redemption; the pages we turn do not become just a bunch of rules that need to be followed out, but the fullness of a story where we become the central characters alongside our Creator.

This takes us to a final point. Let's look at the word *kingdom*. Throughout the gospels, Jesus uses this word over and over when he is teaching the people and his disciples. What he is attempting to explain is that in this world there are two kingdoms co-existing with one another: the kingdom of God, and for a better word, the kingdom of the World (to which Satan is the "prince" of this "kingdom"). He makes it clear and states that each person is in one camp or the other. Jesus says it about as blatantly as it can be said: "If you are not with me, you are against me." (Matthew 12:30) There is no middle ground. Each person is either in allegiance to him or blindly being swayed by his enemy. Even Bob Dylan gets it; in one part of a song he wrote, he belts out this truth:

> You may be an ambassador to England or France
> You may like to gamble, you might like to dance
> You may be the heavyweight champion of the world
> You may be a socialite with a long string of pearls.
>
> Might be a rock'n' roll addict prancing on the stage
> Might have money and drugs at your commands, women in a cage

> You may be a business man or some high degree thief
> They may call you Doctor or they may call you Chief.
>
> You're gonna have to serve somebody, yes indeed
> You're gonna have to serve somebody.
> Well, it may be the devil or it may be the Lord
> But you're gonna have to serve somebody.

The question we each have to ask ourselves is where do we stand, who are we going to serve and follow? Again, there is no middle ground. With this issue, there is never a happy medium. Your mailing address is either in his Kingdom or in the world. You are either for or against Jesus. You are either serving him or someone else. At least, this is how Jesus explained it.

MARKING POINTS THAT WE MAKE

It's good to have an end to journey toward; but it is the journey that matters, in the end. Ursula LeGuin
Never look back unless you are planning to go that way. Henry David Thoreau

And so with all of this, this is why it is important to follow Jesus. Naturally, we are continually being renewed, growing and emerging and becoming more. We need to remember this—our journey of faith has marking points. Being a Christian is a progression. We have many examples of this in Christian literature, *The Pilgrim's Progress* by John Bunyan as the classic and *The Great Divorce* by C.S. Lewis in the last century. And yet, the walk of faith is never one in which the person "arrives." We'll let the eastern religions keep that monopoly. The walk of faith can be likened to one going on a long road trip, crossing state lines and going from one town to the next. Every now and then you may need to stop alongside the road, perhaps to change the tire that has blown or by getting off at the next exit to have some good coffee and a piece of pie at a diner just off the beaten path. Discovery, in the in end, is at the heart of the Christian faith.

Throughout the Bible, God is attempting to pound this idea into us that it's all about a relationship with him that matters the most. The Israelites of the Old Testament had such a hard time with this one, because they wanted so much to make it about following a religion—following a set of rules was so much easier than being in a relationship with their Creator. Very few characters we read about in the Old Testament got this one right. Most, which we read about insisted on obeying all the rules versus moving into a friendship with God. If we were to think about that list of those who moved into an authentic relationship with him, it is a relatively short one. A few would be: Abraham, David, Isaiah, Josiah, and Elijah. When we read their stories, we learn about the beautiful possibilities of having a friendship with God.

In the New Testament, Jesus makes the same challenge. He says that the basis of everything is relationship, a relationship with him. Let's listen to Jesus' all-important words: "I am the vine. You are the branches. He who remains in me, and I in him, the same bears much fruit, for apart from me you can do nothing." (John 15:5) The Message restates it even more emphatically as it ends: "Separated, you can't produce a thing." Now that's saying it like it is! Meditate on that one for a minute. Are we really going to believe such a statement? No one—not your Aunt Bev, not the nice guy down the street who shovels your sidewalk every winter, not even your own mom, the nicest lady in the world—can do anything good without Jesus. What he means in that statement, is simply this—everything has to be about him, otherwise it means nothing. Everything will come up short without Jesus. Every part of our lives must be subject to him: the inner strength of our marriage; the skills and talents we use on the job; our ability in the high school classroom or on the volleyball court; how well we can think or feel; our financial security; our gifts of hospitality or giving; our ability to be a father or mother, son or daughter. Jesus is the center and how centered our lives are to his will determine how well we do in everything that we do. Everything about our lives starts with him. It's not that we don't have importance as well in this ongoing relationship; but the whole of our lives and how we live them starts with the One who made us. *Let me say that one more time: the whole of our lives and how we live them starts with the One who made us.*

This is the starting point and the ending point. Our life, all of it, is in relationship to the One who created us (Colossians 1:16). The closer we are to him, the better we are. I see this continually with my own life and in the lives of others. The better a relationship with God a person has, the more "effectiveness" they have in their own lives. Depression is easier to conquer; marriages re-connect sooner; a father and a teenage son begin to have fun again; sometimes, you can even hit the golf ball straight. Things begin to happen that you never expected to happen. Life begins to fall in place. Inevitably, if we want to have the life we want, if we want to be the person we are supposed to be, it will tie back to our connection with Jesus. In essence, only the person who has God at the center of his life can have the good life. Again, the closer you are to him, the better you will be.

Alongside this, the person who commits his life to God and his ways will go through many changes. Relationships will change. Interests will change. Thinking will change. Life, itself, will change and for the better. If we allow it, the whole of life will just be an on-going metamorphosis into something more, something different, and something good. In the process of the journey, we are inevitably changed. Literally, one year-five years-twenty years later, you'll become an entirely different person, a better person, more sound and connected to something extraordinary. As Muhammed Ali said, "The man who views the world at fifty the same way he did at twenty has wasted thirty years of his life."

THE STAGES WE SEE WITH FAITH

But process inevitably means that there are also stages and I believe that there are different marking points to the Christian walk. It clearly says in the book of Corinthians that in your faith at one point you can be an infant, at another you can be like a child, and then finally, you can live as an adult (1 Corinthians 13:11). Something that I have seen over and over in other people's lives, but most certainly in my own, is that there are three distinct marking points in the Christian walk and it all relates back to our relationship with Jesus.

We hear it all the time: you have to make God No. 1 in your life. Yes, it's a cliché, but even though the phrase is overused, it still is true.

This relationship with God is the key. In speaking of this relationship, it occurred to me that looking back over the last twenty-five years since becoming a Christian I have had differing relationships with him. The relationship changed and grew. Early on, the relationship was more distant, and then gradually has become more intimate. Likewise, I also recognized that Jesus began to play different roles in my life. Just as I was changing in relationship to him; amazingly, he was changing in the way he related to me.

Slowly, but surely, I was living the privilege of a more personal relationship with him. Let me give you an example of how this works. No different than with my seventeen year old son, he has begun to trust me more and I trust him more as well. Josiah is growing up and how I am with him is changing. At one time in his life, he was an infant in which he was entirely dependent on me and I had to do everything for him. As years went by (and much too fast I might add), Josiah grew up into a vivacious and curious nine year old, where now I often had to protect him from himself. And now as he is nearing adulthood, my role as his parent has diminished greatly. He doesn't need me to tell him to tie his shoes, go to bed at the proper time or eat his green beans. Josiah is becoming a mature young man with whom I am very proud. Our relationship has moved from me being a parent to him, to now Josiah has become my friend. In many ways, he doesn't always need my input or protection, because he can take care of himself. In some ways, our relationship with God can be the same. In our own relationship with God, we too can become mature, and become that person to which he also is proud of us.

I began seeing these distinctions, in myself, with others, and in the Scriptures. There were growth spurts to be sure, but in the end, there are three distinct stages in this journey with God. I saw these marking points in the lives of those found in the Old Testament: like Abraham, David, and Elijah. I also saw these steps in the life of the disciples, moving from just-believing to really-living. And finally, as I related the Scriptures to my own life and story, I saw them personally—I had changed and was changing as time went on, growing in my relationship to the One who shaped me together. The progression was marked and obvious. As I began looking back at the years, I saw that not only did I change, but as I mentioned earlier, God also has changed in the way he related to me. Similar in the way a parent relates to a child, the relationship changed and in some ways, we began to relate in different ways. Specifically, I realized that in this journey I moved from being a believer, was transformed into a servant and finally, began to emerge as a friend of Jesus. Perhaps put in another way, God was first my Savior, then became my Lord, and finally became my Friend. This is the transformation I went through and still undergo, each day attempting to move into a friendship with the One who made me for him. By moving closer to Jesus, everything begins to fall in place. Moving forward through this book, this is how we will distinguish these marking points in the journey of being a Christian: a believer, a servant and a friend.

KNOWING WHO YOU SHOULD BE

I want to run; I want to hide; I want to tear down the walls that hold me inside. I want to reach out and touch the flame where the streets have no name. U2

I am not eccentric. It's just that I am more alive than most people. I am an unpopular electric eel set in a pond of goldfish. Edith Sitwell

The end goal of every Christian is to develop a friendship with God. One single passage in the Scriptures is at the heart of this book.

> I'm no longer calling you servants because servants don't understand what their master is thinking and planning.
> No, I've named you friends because I've let you in on everything I've heard from the Father. (John 15:15)

Jesus unmistakably points to the best way to have a relationship with him —in friendship. You find it all in this verse. The question for us is this—how do we get there? In observing it in my own life, I saw that I went through a transformation. I didn't just immediately become friends with God; it culminated, progressed and continues to grow.

By examining your own life, you can find out where you are in your journey with him. I think that this is important for many reasons. First, most importantly, it is imperative that we really assess where we are in our life as related to him. It does no good for us to keep on walking past the mirror and not truly looking into it and seeing what really is in the reflection, whether it is good or not so good. Everything about your life hinges on your relationship with God and so wherever you are in your relationship with him, it's important for you to know in which direction you are moving. We all could say we want something more, something better, but we will never get there, unless we acknowledge where we really are. He also wants more, something better for us.

A friendship with God is obviously where we want to end up, but there were two previous stages in my journey. The first is where it all began. I first became a *believer* in God. Nothing more, nothing less. This was a period in my life in which Jesus was important in my life and sometimes he wasn't. This was a time in my life in which my relationship with God wasn't very personal and it wasn't very passionate or motivated. During that time in my life, I had some very normal, but also some very unique things happen to me which God used to push me along, attempting to draw me further into relationship with him. I will share some of those stories with you so that perhaps in my story you will see your own. One of those experiences was a three-day trip to Toronto. This is when God intervened jealously, and basically challenged me to put up or shut up. That's when I decided that to be a *servant*, a learner; a follower of Jesus was of all-importance and was where I needed to go. The Scriptures speak often to the point that God gets envious for his children and in my own life, he was single-minded about me. At that time, he voiced loudly and clearly that he wanted all of my life or nothing of it. To that point, at different times in my life, he would grab me by the shirt and pull me in the direction of his choosing. Obviously in these moments, this wasn't always easy or enjoyable. But it was good, because where I was headed was not a place that I would want to end up and he knew that.

In years following this period of my life, I learned how to be a follower and servant, attempting every day to let him have run of my life. But this was not the end. Even this had its obstacles and problems, and God began to draw them out. The two areas which were hindering me was my own personal healing and connected to this, genuinely knowing his grace and forgiveness in my life. Down into my very soul, he showed me that while I maybe was able to mouth the words *Amazing Grace*, I really wasn't singing them. Jesus in his own way was saying to me, *I know longer wish to call you a servant—I have something better for you. Will you still follow now?* Some years later, I slowly began to learn that being friends with God was entirely different than just being his servant. This inevitably brought me into a unique friendship with him. Again, in upcoming chapters I will share how this happened for me and how you too maybe need to take that journey as well.

The age-old question that always gets asked at some point or another is this —who am I? When one becomes a friend of Jesus, one begins to ask a better question. It's not necessary to ask who I am from my own perspective—the best question is—who does God say that I am. It's an easy thing to know who we are; it's a much different thing to know who we should be. You will never really know who you are until you realize where you belong and the most important place where you belong is in a friendship with God. Giving yourself over to this will lead you into a wild and wonderful relationship with a Father who has something up his sleeve for your life.

THE JOURNEY WE MUST ALL MAKE

Are you paralyzed with fear? That's a good sign. Fear is good. Like self-doubt, fear is an indicator. Fear tells us what we have to do. Remember our rule of thumb: The more scared we are of a work or calling, the more sure we can be that we have to do it. Resistance is experienced as fear; the degree of fear equates the strength of Resistance. Therefore, the more fear we feel about a specific enterprise, the more certain we can be that that enterprise is important to us and to the growth of our soul.
Steven Pressfield

But for us the road unfurls itself, we don't stop walking, we know there is far to go.
Denise Levertov

There are some givens you and I must agree on as we explore each stage, our development from a believer to a disciple and then to a friend of God. First, by looking at someone else's life we can also see our own. We will begin by briefly looking at the lives of three people in the New Testament, Judas, Peter and Barnabas, and we will see these stages come alive and perhaps be able to see ourselves in their stories. I will also integrate my own story, as I am no different than you. I will share how God has always been after me, pushing me to come closer to Him. This is how He is with everyone. By hearing some of my story, perhaps, you will be able to hear your own. By looking at some of these steps, I believe, we can discover not only who we are, but who we are to become.

Second, these three stages of *believer, servant* and *friend* are distinct and it is important that you begin to look at your own life and see where you are, but then also find out where you've come from. What is your journey been like? It is distinct and your own and you must discover those special features. God deals with each of us individually and in his own way. There are ways he relates to me that make sense to me, but wouldn't make sense to you and vice-versa. This uniqueness of relationship is illustrated in a striking manner in the book of Revelation. It shares that when we see Jesus face-to-face, he will give each of us a stone. Written on this small stone will be your unique name, which only you and he will know (Revelation 2:17). This is incredible if you think about it. This is how incomparable and exceptional you are and how distinct your relationship is to Him. God singles each of us out. It's important that you really think about this; you have your own story and Jesus is persuading you to come along into something that will not only just transform you today, but your future as well.

You must also understand that moving you through these stages of spiritual growth are something that God does, but it is also something that you must do. Each of these steps requires you to make a decision and then act on that choice. I decided to become a *believer* in Jesus. I decided to become a *servant* of Jesus. I decided to become a *friend* of Jesus. You must do the same. There are no special gimmicks you have to follow; there are no hoops you have to jump through; there isn't any conference you can attend. A relationship with God is a hand-in-hand experience—he holding on to us and we grabbing on for dear life to Him. God never forces us to be in relationship with him and therefore, some of the responsibility lies with us. He woos us, but we must follow. So often, he says—*Come, follow me*—but he never demands it. It's always a request. I am convinced beyond a shadow of a doubt that this is exactly where God wants us to be—in a reciprocal friendship with him where both parties are invested. This is his greatest desire and he wants us to follow, because he knows all that is in store for both of us.

Finally, and this may seem odd and contradictory, but this is not a book about trying to get through the "steps." Growing in friendship with God is always a natural process. It's a day by day process and it will last the rest of your life. Each day you must decide, "Will I be a believer, will I be a servant or will I be a friend to Jesus today?" Likewise, this is not a book at about becoming religious or spiritual. It's about coming into a relationship with the One who created you and desires to know you at an intimate level.

TAKING A LONG LOOK IN THE MIRROR

If anything, you have to be honest with yourself and be where you are at in your life. As an example of this, whenever, someone pursues counseling in their life, and they have come because of a certain problem, I always tell them that half the battle had been won—that they will most likely overcome their obstacles, because they have acknowledged them. They have admitted where they are. This is exactly what we need to do through this process. God desires our honesty and we need to be straightforward with ourselves. We need to come to the place where we can honestly assess where our relationship with God is today.

So where are you in your walk with God? Have you been a Christian for 30 years, and yet really you are no different than you were when you were fourteen when you went to the altar at the Bible camp? Is your relationship with God in word only? That's okay. Admit it. Take off the masks. Come clean with those around you. Most importantly, do this with yourself and move on, and become a follower of Jesus, giving all of your life to him and not just parts of you or the fringes of your life. If you are a friend of Jesus already—great—but the journey is not over. Continue to be his companion, but even more so, continue hard after him, striving to develop that friendship more and more each day. Again, remember no matter how close you are to God, each day you must get up, and make a decision—will I be a believer, a servant or a friend of Jesus today. Some days are better than others; some days you will venture forth into untraveled territory, and on other days you will go back from where once you came.

A while back someone at our church gave me a framed picture for my office. At the bottom, it reads, "Courage does not always roar. Sometimes courage is the quiet voice at the end of the day saying, 'I will try again tomorrow.'" I like that. Some days are better than others—some days we regress, others we push on. But it all boils down to a decision, and every day we must make it. A. W. Tozer said it just right when he wrote:

> Knowledge of such a Being cannot be gained by study alone. It comes by a wisdom the natural man knows nothing of, neither can know, because it is spiritually discerned. To know God is at once the easiest and the most difficult thing in the world. It is easy because the knowledge is not won by hard mental toil, but it is something freely given. As sunlight falls free on the open field, so the knowledge of the holy God is a free gift to men who are open to receive it.

Those are the operative words—*those who are open to receive it*. Again, you need to look at where you are in their life, assess where you want to go, and then finally, move in that direction. Are you open to becoming a friend of Jesus? Or does the status quo suit you just fine? Jesus says come closer and you will see that where you are now in your life is but a paltry and flat existence compared to what he has planned for you.

These next words might be the most important in the whole of what I am writing. You are sitting here reading this by yourself. Usually, when we read something, we do it alone. But this book was written with the thought that it wouldn't be just something that was read, but that it would be something that was done. We all have been guilty of just reading books, blogs or other stuff. They help us get our mind off things; they entertain us; they inform us. However, books or other writings are not meant to be just read; they were meant to be applied. Again, this is a book to be done. Do your best to keep this commitment. Often when doing something alongside learning about it, something happens in our mind and it takes—it moves from something that we know to something that we understand. To understand something means to get under it, and really see it for what it is and to apply that information. By doing this, often there is a connection that occurs—through the words we learn and by our actions a change can occur that will last for the rest of our lives. Slow down with this process, read the book slowly (you don't have to get through it in a week). Rather take time and make it a time to listen to the One who maybe has something to say to you.

Think about it this way—in psychology, we like to talk about two types of change: first and second order change. *First order change* occurs when something is transformed for just a short time. It's a momentary shift or temporary adjustment. We see this all the time, the guy who has the drinking problem is able to control it for a little while, but three years later he regresses, falls away and slides back into his old ways. Maybe for a few weeks, miraculously maybe for a few months, we change different attitudes, thoughts or behaviors. However, after that, we revert back to our old selves. This type of change is not what we are after.

Then there is *second order change*. This is what we are after—this is our goal at the end of the day when we try to modify our life. Second order change is permanent, cannot be interrupted and is impossible to change back. When it comes to the crucial stuff in life, it is my conviction that only Jesus can bring about second order change—change that is locked in and unable to be altered. What areas of our life might this be? It could be how a marriage or a family behaves. It could be a struggle with lust, bitterness, or rage. It could simply be how one views God or themselves. Second order change not only gives us a new way of looking at things, but offers us a new story. We literally become new people. This is exactly what happens when we apply truths to our life so that we can get at the change that is for good and will last.

LEARNING BY DOING

You can read all the manuals on prayer and listen to other people pray, but until you begin to pray yourself you will never understand prayer. It's like riding a bicycle or swimming: You learn by doing.
　　　　　　　　　　Luis Palau

This is what we are after, isn't it? We want change. However, we want the real thing as well. Be entirely honest with yourself, are you the same person you were a year ago? Five years ago? Forty years ago? This might possibly be the greatest danger in being a Christian.

Along these lines, I once heard a pastor say this, *Trust this Jesus—this all you need to do.* Maybe he misspoke, but that was completely an untrue statement. This is what so many people are told when they come to faith and it only gives them permission to continue to be the fallen individuals they are, not growing and not changing into the incredible people they were meant to be. Being in relationship with Jesus goes way beyond just trusting. So really dwell on this question—are you any different than you used to be?

- Is anger always at your side and comes out whenever it wants?
- What about the inability to overcome the continual depression and joylessness?
- Or the art you've acquired to being committed to absolutely nothing or anyone?
- Or the perpetual lying and half-truths?
- Or the endless relationships you've had that go about an inch deep?
- Or wasting your life away with procrastination or laziness?
- Or the past that always stands between you and where you want to go?
- Or how you allow shopping or sex (or anything else other than

God) make you feel secure and happy?

We could go on and on with these kinds of examples. This would be a great time to take a moral inventory and really look at your life. Again, being a Christian on one level is about constant change. Are you a sinner? Of course you are. Just like me. And this is exactly why God is always at us to become more, more in terms of who He desires us to be—more whole today, sinning less tomorrow, and becoming just a little bit more like Jesus. Let's make no bones about it, this is no simple or easy task, but this is what we must be after—we need to everyday become different people than who we were from the previous day.

This is why change happens in large part because we do something to bring about that change. This reminds me of a story. The very first client I ever had came into my office, sat in the chair and demanded in no uncertain terms that she didn't think she was going to get very much out of this "counseling thing." I think I might have surprised her, because I agreed with her. I said to her that she was probably right—in a certain way. I explained to her that this time that we shared together was most likely going to only make a small impact on her life. What she did outside of the time that we met—this was what was going to make all the difference. It's exactly the same here. Simply learning about the different stages of the Christian walk will do absolutely nothing for you. Knowledge is just knowledge unless it's applied to one's life. Too often books or things we read just become information to us and not much else. Jesus wants us to have more than the facts. Again, everything will depend on what you do with the information that you will read.

Another point to be made is this—often when you are attempting to do something that is challenging, it is best to have someone else's help. This book was written, first and foremost, to be utilized in the context of community, in which, people come clean about where they are and who they are and then delve deep within themselves. This is a book about running with one another toward a deeper relationship with God and no matter where you are at in your journey, anyone can benefit from this. The key point in that last sentence is the words with one another. This is no self-help book. If anything, it's all about "group-help." Remember, it's not about who gets to the finish line first, because there is no finish line. Again, it's a paradox. We are made as individuals, but at the same time and quite unique to our faith; we were made as a community, a family, a nation, a tribe. This may be for you the first objective, and that is to find a small group of friends to join you in this journey.

Let me make one final word at this point. Throughout this writing I am going to be labeling these three distinct relationships that we can have with God; they are unique words which have distinct meanings: *believer, servant* and *friend*. Unique to this book, most often when reading a Christian book or blog, the use of the words believer and servant are usually positive ones. I fully agree that these can be good terms to characterize a person who is a Christian. However, for the purpose of this book, they most often will be used as negative terms. In the end, God wants us to be his friend, not just a believer and not just a servant. As Jesus clearly shows he wants more from us and as he directly says I no longer call you servants, instead I have called you friend. (John 15:15) Let me end this section by briefly offering definitions to these distinctions that hopefully will fill in your understanding of what we will be talking about throughout the book. In the following chapters, we will fully explore what each of these are all about:

- *Believer*: A person who just believes in God, but does not actively follow him. "Believing" in this case is simply giving mental assent to a religion or creed—this is the person who has very little conviction about what it means to be a follower of Jesus Christ. Oftentimes, these are people who have grown up in a church (Catholic or Protestant), but have never fully given their lives over to God and applied the Bible to their lives. A term you may have heard that would apply here is "nominal Christian." A nominal

Christian is one who says that they are a Christian, but rarely goes to church or is someone who selects "Christianity" as their religion, but would also say they are "non-practicing." Examples of characters in the Bible who would be characterized as believers would be: Esau, Saul, Solomon (toward the end of his life), Ahab, and Judas.

- *Servant*: A person who has gone beyond just believing in Jesus, but bases their relationship with God on rules and what they think is being a good Christian. This person may know a tremendous amount of "stuff" about God, but practically speaking, does not know Him personally and has not genuinely experienced three important aspects; these would be grace, genuine self-forgiveness and personal healing for trouble spots in their lives (e.g., anger, sexual addictions, depression, etc.). These people are easily bound by legalism, because they have not experienced this grace and freedom. People caught in this phase of faith often use religion to their benefit, are very adept at hiding problems in their lives, and sometimes are church leaders. The two clearest examples of this type of person would be the religious leaders, the Pharisees that Jesus would often challenge and confront and as we will explore in detail in the book, the character of Peter that we read about in the gospels (before Jesus' resurrection).
- *Friend*: A person who has undergone a transformation and is beginning to know healing, maturity and the freedom of following Christ. They can genuinely say, *I know grace down into my bones*. This person is beginning to hear the voice of the One they follow (John 10:27) and graciously encourages others to do likewise. This person looks carefully in the mirror at their lives and seeks out healing for the wounds that have occurred to them and the brokenness that they have brought into their lives. Those

who have become friends of Jesus are not bound by rules, but through the Spirit live lives which are characterized by the fruit of the Spirit (Galatians 5:22-23). Those that we find in the Bible that we would characterize as being friends with God would include: Abraham, Joseph, Moses, David, Elijah, Ruth, Peter (after Jesus' resurrection), Barnabas, and Priscilla.

PART TWO

JUST BELIEVING IN GOD

THE QUINTESSENTIAL BELIEVER – JUDAS

This is a fictitious short story written about a moment in the life of Judas from the perspective of one of the twelve disciples, Bartholomew. It exemplifies the reality of what Judas maybe was like, following Jesus at a distance.

Granted, it had been a long day. There hadn't been rain for weeks and it was very dusty. We were coated with dirt. It was in our hair, under our fingernails and we needed to wash, but that wasn't going to happen for many more days. We had been on the road for a long time and many of us were weary and restless. In particular, Judas seemed to be more defensive, short, even angry, especially toward Jesus and for some reason, toward Peter as well. Judas was usually quiet, hanging in the background and only really speaking up when it had to do with something that pertained to the money or where we would go next. This was different.

You see, Judas took care of the coin that we got and Jesus trusted him. When we would go into the towns, Judas would seek out our lodging, figure out where we would eat, and take care of the practical things that needed to be done. He would only on occasion be there when Jesus would be teaching at the synagogue or at the different times we would spend with the people teaching them or helping them. It was odd though, because now looking back in hindsight, Judas didn't really spend very much time with us at all. He was most of the time off doing his own thing.

That day though I knew something was up. Again, we were dirty and tired and the people were just wearing on most of us. They wanted so much; they thronged around us all the time; they were always in your face. On some days that could give you strength and excitement for what was happening, but on that day, I think we were all just plain tired. We went back to the place where we were staying, which that night meant that we were sleeping outside. The last few days Jesus would go to Judas and ask him if we had enough money to sleep under a roof. Each time, early in the day when Jesus would ask him about this, Judas said that we would either stay dry or go hungry. We had to choose if we wanted to eat or sleep. At those time, we wondered where was all of the money going. Was Judas just giving it away?

On that day, it wasn't until early evening that Jesus went to Judas again and asked him about the money and where we might stay. Like I said, it'd been a long day and we were all aching from our travels. Judas though lost his temper. Jesus didn't have but a few words out of his mouth, and Judas threw the money pouch at him and the money struck Jesus in the face and then it all fell to the ground—just a few silver coins staring back at him. Then, this was the remarkable thing—Judas who was quite a bit smaller than Jesus, went at him as if he was going to strike him with his fist. We stood amazed. Right before his fist was about to land, he pulled back and uttered something which none of us could hear. Later that night, as we were all sitting around the fire and most everyone else had gone to sleep, those of us who were still awake asked one another if they had heard what Judas had said. None of us did. After Judas did pull back his fist and said what he had to say, he walked off mumbling down the road toward Bethlehem.

No one had spoken to Jesus like that, even those who detested him like some of the synagogue leaders just said things behind his back. They never confronted him to his face. A lot of us were confused. And what was going on? Did others have the same feelings as Judas? We didn't believe that Judas would come back; and that he was gone for good. But the next morning, very early, he was trotting down the road as we had just finished eating. Nothing was said. Jesus didn't bring it up and Judas acted like nothing had happened. I remember that day well, because I finally began to figure out who Judas really was. As usual, at about midday, there was another great throng of people eager to hear what Jesus had to say and to see what he would do. There were people everywhere —pushing and shoving to get close to him. However, as I looked through the crowd, this is what I saw—Judas was mixing among the people, collecting coins from them, and pushing the change into his pockets. For the first time, things became clear to me, and when I looked over to Jesus, he simply nodded to me—that's when I knew he had seen what I had seen.

IT'S AN EASY THING TO BELIEVE IN GOD

Our critical day is the not the very day of our death; but the whole course of our life. I thank him that prays for me when my bell tolls, but I thank him much more who instructs me how to live.

John Donne

In the space between yes and no, there's a lifetime. It's the difference between the path you walk and the one you leave behind; it's the gap between who you thought you could be and who you really are; its the legroom for the lies you'll tell yourself in the future.

Jodi Picoult

In any journey, you have to start somewhere. Believing in Jesus also has a beginning. Whatever you want to call it—giving your life to God, being born-again, finding Jesus—the Christian journey starts off by believing. A believer is someone…well…who believes. How does a dictionary describe belief? It defines the word as simply the mental act, condition or habit of placing trust or confidence in a person or thing. Sounds pretty easy, doesn't it? I like to think of it as a change of mind. I once thought this; now I see it this way. This is what believing is—it's a little more than changing your mind.

As an example, a case in point of this occurred in our home many years ago when we introduced our two sons to the food from Thailand. It is by far the food that Julie and I enjoy the most. When we lived in Chicago, we would have it delivered every Friday night—an order of Pad Thai and Pad See Ew. Up to that point, the most risqué thing our boys had eaten was something called the Ultradog—a unique and messy hot dog from a place here in Grand Rapids called Yesterdog. It's coated with onions, chili, cucumber shavings, and ketchup and mustard (yeah, I know it sounds disgusting, but you've got to try one). So one Saturday evening, we decided to introduce some Thai dishes to our sons. Micah, at the time was probably five, and immediately and emphatically expressed his disapproval. "Yuck, no way! Gross!" After finally getting him to the restaurant (yanking and pulling and bribing) and then finally making him take a bite, he bellowed, "Hmmm…This Thai food doesn't taste half bad!" His mind and taste buds had been transformed. He changed his mind about how good Thai food actually was. Put simply, he began to believe in the goodness of Thai food.

Believing in God on one level is similar and is a pretty simple process if you think about it. Whether you are a thirteen year old at a Bible camp or the chief of some long-lost tribe in Kenya who's never even seen a book, let alone a Bible, the process is no different:

- You understand that God exists.
- Your life is confronted about who you are through the story of the cross.
- You acknowledge who you are as a sinner and who God is as a Redeemer.
- You begin to believe in God and begin to believe that He can forgive and absolve your sins.

God made it easy and straight forward in starting a relationship with him. For some of us, it happened when mom came in our room when we were six and prayed for us at our bedtime and then asked us if we wanted "Jesus to come into our heart." For some others, it happened in high school or college, an arduous intellectual process in which we needed all the facts lined up, and all the apologetics made straight in our mind, and we then made a mental transformation in our belief system. And then, for some of us, we were deep in our own broken world, had made a total mess of our lives, maybe we were going from bed to bed or from drink to drink, and saw only one way out and that was the way of Jesus. Believers come in all different shapes and sizes; perhaps they have been Christians for forty days or as long as forty years.

There are many ways in which God reaches out to each of us. He is often imaginative in his approach. Jesus is so in love with us that he will do whatever it takes to be near us, close to us, in relationship with us. There are many ways in which he captivates us and I have heard countless stories and the many different ways in which people come to faith.

- A camp counselor tells you about this captivating Person and you want to know him.
- A guy hands you a tract on the subway.
- It's late at night, you can't sleep because of a head cold, and you're flipping through the channels and you come upon some television preacher.
- You are all alone in another town on a business trip for three days and on the second day you open up the bed stand table and begin flipping through the book that lies there.
- A friend opens up their life to you about Someone who has made a dramatic difference in their life.

As I once heard Joseph Stowell comment, "God is like the Royal Canadian Mounted Police…He always get his man." And in doing so, God comes up with some of the most normal and most odd ways in bridging that gap—from not believing at all in him, to at least believing just a little bit.

A DREAM LIKE NO OTHER

There is every excuse for blundering in the dark, but in the light there is no cover from reality. It is because we strongly sense this, and not merely because we feel that the evidence is ancient and scanty, that we shrink from committing ourselves to such a far-reaching belief that Jesus Christ was really God.

J. B. Phillips

God doesn't want something from us. He simply wants us.

C.S. Lewis

One of the more interesting ways in which a friend of mine began his life as a Christian was through an exceptional dream. Back when I was in college, I met Shunyuan; he was from Taiwan and was in his residency to become a physician at the University of Illinois in Chicago. Shunyuan began attending our little Bible study that we held into the wee hours of a Friday night—just a couple of 20-somes who were hanging out and talking about the Scriptures as it pertained to our motley lives. Shunyuan had grown up Buddhist and I wasn't ever quite sure why he would show up each time we met—if you aren't a Christian, taking your Friday night to study the Bible I would guess isn't on too many people's lists. Shunyuan's beliefs were different than ours and he let us know that, and yet each Friday he would show up and be ready to share his own thoughts, often asking us really good questions on why we followed this person Jesus. Even though he had grown up religious, at the heart of it, he was an atheist. He really did not believe anything. That was okay for us; we needed someone to challenge our own thoughts and ideas, and he would often have some good stuff for us to think about.

However, this unbelief all changed one night. One morning he woke up out of a beautiful and terrible sleep, and his life was entirely altered. Shunyuan had a dream one fall night that dramatically changed him and altered his life. He recounted a couple of days later to us that in this dream he was swimming in the ocean with his daughter who was about six at the time. Shunyuan's daughter meant everything to him and was the one thing that did bring him great joy and meaning to his life. When we would openly share about our lives, a couple of different times, Shunyuan would tell us that he would not know what to do if something ever happened to her. His daughter was the center of his life.

In this dream, his daughter and him were swimming in the ocean, and out of nowhere, a shark attacks his daughter, tearing at her right arm. Shunyuan pulls her ashore and as he sees the blood pouring from her arm, as a doctor he knows that if he does not tend to her quickly, she will bleed to death. He sees how dire the situation is and he grows pale because there is no way to stop the bleeding. The love of his life is going to die and he begins to weep. As he looks up, he sees a man walking toward them. A strange thing happens: immediately, he recognizes that this person is Jesus and as he fixes his eyes on him, Shunyuan realizes immediately that Jesus knows his true heart—that Shunyuan does not want to have anything to do with him. Again, because of this, he becomes hopeless because he believes that Jesus will not heal his daughter, which now he believes and knows that he can do. In the dream, Shunyuan envisions that Jesus will just continue to walk down the beach and do nothing to help him.

However, Jesus does the opposite of everything that Shunyuan believes and he walks up to his daughter and kneels next to her. Jesus touches her arm and everything is restored, healing her completely. Without looking back at Shunyuan, Jesus then wanders off down the beach without a word.

As we were on the edge of our seats listening to his story, Shunyuan told us that right after this he woke from his dream. As he was waking from his sleep, he was taken aback from the dream—at that moment, in the early morning, he decided to give his life to this Jesus.

Shunyuan began to "believe" that Jesus was the Savior, his Savior and that he really could do remarkable things.

This is often how believing begins, we see that God is good and we begin to trust him just a little bit. No different than what happened to Shunyuan, this is how God often moves into our lives—he whispers to us who he really is.

IS THIS JUST A PHASE?

> *One is happy as a result of one's own efforts once one knows the necessary ingredients of happiness: simple tastes, a certain degree of courage, self denial to a point, love of work, and above all, a clear conscience.* George Sand
>
> *If you want a religion that makes sense, I would suggest something other than Christianity. If you want a religion that makes life, this is the one.* Rich Mullins

So what exactly are the characteristics of a believer? We will go over some tale-tale signs of the person who just believes in God, but doesn't take it much farther than that. The day that a person comes to believe that Jesus is their Savior is a beautiful, yet dangerous moment. It's wonderful because it starts life off in a way in which we begin again. The words to portray this experience can range from cleansing to newness to freedom. It's a unique experience unlike anything that we will ever undergo. Think about it for minute—at one point, you are entirely alienated from the Creator of the universe to now being his child. That is one remarkable transformation!

And it can happen in the blink of an eye: on a deathbed, at a rock concert, in the bathroom while taking a shower, in the front seat while talking to a friend, late one night in front of the TV. At some unique point, we decide to believe that Jesus Christ is the Savior of the world. Everyone comes into relationship with God in so many different ways. My paternal grandfather was a perfect example of this. For some reason, and I don't know the whole story, he became a Christian some time in his seventies. To be honest, he drove everyone bonkers because of this magnificent change. He was always talking about God; going to church every Sunday morning and evening and every Wednesday after dinner; writing large checks to different ministries like Billy Graham's or to the

Lutheran Church to which he belonged. My grandfather let you know that he was a Christian. He had his tracts that he would hand out to guests who would visit. He preached fire and brimstone as well as any preacher I've heard since (this is not necessarily a good thing). He had this dramatic turnaround in his life that he wanted others to share in as well. His intentions were most likely pure, but I'm not sure about his presentation because in the end, he didn't sway anyone to his side. In fact, he might have pushed people away.

You see, I always knew my grandfather as a very kind man, sitting on his knee, listening to his fishing stories and eating slices of fresh apple. But my dad and others, knew him when he wasn't so nice or pleasant to be around. They knew him as a father who could be tough and overly strict. They knew him as a hard man. They knew someone who was far from being a saint. This change confused them, I think because they wondered if the change would be permanent. My grandfather didn't live relatively long after giving his life to God and so I think this also was where some mistrust came, because those around him never really got a chance to find out if his changed life was was really going to stick or if he was going to revert back to the person they once knew—that guy who wasn't always so easy to be around.

This is the problem with believers, one just never knows if this is just a phase or something long-lasting in their life. We all have heard stories of those who passionately give their life to God, serve relentlessly in the church, and yet a few years later, they can't be found. We have all heard stories of those who once were pastors, deacons or serving in some capacity of leadership, and got caught in adultery or some other indiscretion and haven't been seen since. The reason it is so dangerous to stay just a believer is because one's relationship with God is based on something very flimsy and that is, it's simply based on a belief. This may sound funny, but later on, when one makes deeper commitments, one's connection to God is not simply founded on belief or faith, but also will be based on experience and a personal relationship with God. Jesus wants to be in every nook and cranny of our lives and with that, we can experience him in many directions and dimensions in our lives. Jesus desires to be experienced, and typically, the believer has few events in his life in which God truly seems real and alive in their lives. If you were to ask a believer if God really existed; they at least eighty percent of the time would just shrug their shoulders. Believers don't know God exists; they hope so. This is exactly the conundrum where Judas found himself. Do you really believe that Judas would sell out the Savior of the world for a mere thirty pieces of silver, and at the same time, truly believe in his heart that Jesus was the actual Messiah? Of course, not. Judas betrayed Jesus because he wasn't certain and positive that Jesus was telling the truth about himself. This is where the story about the guy who builds his house on sand comes in—Jesus is maintaining that we need to have a deeper relationship with him, something that can withstand doubt or tragedy (Matthew 7:26). The problem is, believers don't do this. They are building on the beach, right next to the ocean as the waves come closer.

GIVING 100%

We never become truly spiritual by sitting down and wishing to become so. You must undertake something so great that you cannot accomplish it unaided. Phillips Brooks

Our compromises, not our achievements, define us. Hal Croves

In the Old Testament, it says that God delighted in David and loved him dearly (2 Samuel 22). Even though David committed adultery, had someone killed and did a pretty awful job at raising his children, God had a special place for David in his heart. Do you know why that was? It was because David lived his life entirely God-centered even when he messed up. His life is a testimony that no matter what you've done, God will never abandon you. In this dedication to God, he lived his life as if he was at his side at all times. God was really real to David. Just look at the Psalms. David was thankful to God for everything in his life and we can find that gratefulness in the songs of the Bible. David gave God credit for everything good that happened to him. David saw His hand in every aspect of his life. I am sure that often people would roll their eyes with the stories David would tell. Why did he always have to give God the credit? Couldn't he just realize that not every good thing came from God's hand and that sometimes he himself made the great things happen? Couldn't he see that he was just plain lucky or like most of us, was making a good life by pulling up his boots straps and making it happen? But David acknowledged the Lord in every way. Because of this, David gave his all to God, because he saw him in every facet of his life.

Now think of Judas. When we read the gospels, it seems to hint that Judas wasn't around very much. As you later read about how Judas betrays Jesus, you begin to wonder how much he really was around during those three years that they knew one another. I imagine Judas was at his side when it was convenient or necessary, but when it counted, he was most likely nowhere to be found. Perhaps when Jesus was directly teaching and there was an opportunity for him to learn something, he was off doing his own thing. What Jesus was doing was just a waste of time.

Money was to be made for the "ministry," he might have argued. We know that from the gospels that Judas was the treasurer of Jesus' band of followers and that he took some of the money for himself. (John 13:29) When a person begins to compromise, break the rules a bit, one's relationship to God gets splintered and slowly, but surely you begin to compromise in multiple areas of your life. With this, it made it all the easier for Judas to betray Jesus, and betray him to the priests. Judas was like the church at Laodecia that we learn about in the book of Revelation, neither hot nor cold. (Revelation 3:14-18) Judas was wishy-washy and that's typically what believers are—neither here nor there and they often keep God at a distance.

As we can see clearly in Judas' life, it can be dangerous to stay a believer. Throughout the gospels, Jesus firmly maintains that he wants all or nothing. Think about that—he wants all of you or nothing of you. He would rather not have us at all, unless he has all of us. When it comes to this, Jesus is an extremist when it applies to our relationship with him. As Jim Eliot exclaimed, "Oh that God would make us dangerous!" This is what we need. To be completely given over—we need to journey into deeper commitment that becomes precarious to live out, because we live at the edge of ourselves. This is where David lived his life and it was rich. Judas took another way, an easier way, and in the end, he lost everything.

Here is the big question that you have to ask: does God have all of you? Does he own every aspect of your life:
- Your relationships
- Your work and career
- Your family and kids

- Your money and finances
- Your decisions about your future

Likewise, who makes the decisions in your life—you or God? Who determines:

- The friendships you keep.
- The person you will marry.
- What you will study in college.
- What job you will pursue.
- Which neighborhood you live in.
- What you buy at Best Buy or at Amazon.
- The car you drive.
- What you do with your free time.

Another good question for you to ask—when a good thing happens in your life who gets the credit—you or God? Remember every good thing comes from his hand. Do you live that out, speak that out, and acknowledge that on a fairly regular basis? On the reverse, when a bad thing happens in your life, who gets that credit—you or God? The irony is that often we hear people blame God for the bad things that happen to them even though 99% percent of the time they have had nothing to do with him in the first place. They've been the ones living and orchestrating their lives, but when something hard hits them, their first words are—where was God? Where was God when I lost my job (when in reality, I was doing really sloppy work)? Where was God when my boyfriend broke up with me (when I shouldn't have been with him in the first place)? Where was God when I had to file bankruptcy (when in truth, I was spending money left and right)? This is often where believers live their lives—living on their own, not giving credit when credit is due, and then when trials occur, they play the blame game. If these are some of your patterns, you probably are just a believer and as we will discover, there is actually a better way.

HIDE AND SEEK

The measure of a man's real character is what he would do if he knew he would never be found out.

Thomas Macaulay

Frightful this is in a sense, but it is true, and every one who has merely some little knowledge of the human heart can verify it: there is nothing to which a man holds so desperately as to his sin.

Søren Kierkegaard

Judas liked to hide who he really was. As an example, in the gospel of John, it tells us that he would take money and conceal that from Jesus and the others (John 12:6). You can picture Judas taking a few extra coins out of a pouch and secretly placing them in his left pocket. Later on, he would go off without anyone knowing and go spend his little stolen fortune. Perhaps he would go off with a prostitute and take bliss in the secrets of the night or go off and dine alone with some food that was more to his taste as the disciples ate the same thing day after day—some unleavened bread and fish. It was second nature for Judas to conceal who he really was.

Believers typically like to hide too. In my own life, when I was in college and had just become a Christian, I can remember scampering past my friend Greg's door, concealing a bottle of wine, praying he would not open that door and catch me with that burgundy bottle hidden under my trench coat. Greg had led me to my faith and I didn't want him to know I was still really struggling—with drinking, staying up until the wee hours of the night smoking pot, sleeping with my girlfriend, etc., etc., etc. During that spring semester, often I wore a mask around him, presenting a person who wasn't the real me. When around him, I would always play a part as if I was some Oscar winner in a film. I played it well and fooled most of those around me. In the end, they never really knew the whole story.

But during those early college years, I did know who I really was, and it was hard living that way. I was still very scared to show who I really was and to be honest, I really didn't want to change anyway. On the one hand, Christians seemed very loving and kind to one another, but in comparison to my life, their lives seemed rather drab and boring. This is what I thought, anyway. My life seemingly had an excitement to it and that was very hard to give up. At the same time, it was also very tiring and difficult to live that way on a day-to-day basis.

Those who just believe are always playing these two roles. It is the Jekyll and Hyde syndrome. If you've seen *The Lord of the Rings* trilogy in the theaters or read the J.R. Tolkien's books, believers are like the character of Golem—one day all smiles and the next, wearing a mean and vicious face. On some days, believers are true to themselves and their convictions and on others, they let loose and do as they please. As this continues to go on and they live in these two realms, slowly, but surely, they will begin to play a part—the character of the "Christian." Believers who stay believers too long end up only playing a part or role. Proper haircut: check. Bible in hand: check. Smile on my face: check. No cuss words: check. Religious talk: check. You get what I mean? It can be so easy to play the part of the Christian, and yet fool everyone, even ourselves. But this stuff is not what a relationship with God is based on, is it?

And the even greater danger is this—unless we come clean to someone about what we are struggling with, who we really are behind closed doors—often we will continue to go to church, perhaps even be involved, but we will do everything we can do to hide who we really are. This then becomes the real you; the person you hide from everyone:

- I lie all the time about my accomplishments and past. I exaggerate a lot.

- I am always screaming at my kids. They often have looks of terror on their faces.
- In truth, I despise my husband and do not love him any longer. I have been flirting with the guy who sits near me at work.
- I've been doing cocaine with a guy from work—only two people know about this side of my life (me and him).
- Late at night, when everyone's asleep, I surf the web for porn. When the credit card statements come, I quickly pay them off so that no one will know.
- I know it—one day soon, I'm going to just haul off and hit my wife.
- I tell some of my friends' really awful things about someone we know. I don't know if any of it is true.
- Me and some friends have been cheating on our exams this semester. It's easy. I'd know this stuff if I would study, so what's the harm?
- My girlfriend and I have been having sex at her parent's house when they're gone.
- I've been having suicidal thoughts. I recently bought a gun.
- I've lost $5,000 gambling in the last six months and my husband doesn't know.
- I've been stealing money from my roommate.
- I can't stop thinking about having sex with a co-worker. We're both men.

This is a very perilous place to be because as we keep this life hidden, everything underneath will begin to fester, and then it will become more and more difficult to reveal the real you—to genuinely come forward about those weaknesses and sins in our lives. In the end, we will just be playing a role to which we get better and better at playing. We may even win awards and adulations, but as for the real us, we know who that person really is.

SOMETIMES THINGS AREN'T WHAT THEY SEEM

It is the characteristic excellence of the strong man that he can bring momentous issues to the fore and make a decision about them. The weak are always forced to decide between alternatives they have not chosen themselves.
Dietrich Bonhoeffer

The breaking of a wave cannot explain the whole sea. Vladimir Nabokov

When I was about eleven years old, we made our first trip as a family out to Delaware which we continue even to this day. It was a remarkable and magical vacation for me. It was the first time I tasted salt water taffy. The first time I went clamming and crabbing. And most importantly, the first time I swam in the ocean. I will never forget that summer and I will tell you one of the reasons why. When it came to vacations, we had a tradition in our family. On long trips, my mom would take me to Kroger and I could get a mess of magazines or books, which she hoped would keep me busy on the long car ride. I remember vividly what I chose the day before we left on that trip. I got a bunch of books on sharks and shark attacks.

We lived just south of Chicago and I think by the time we had made it through Ohio, I had read each book—cover to cover—all four of them. When we reached Delaware, I fell in love with the ocean—I had never seen it before and I couldn't wait to jump in. Each day of the vacation that week, that's where you find me—swimming in its waters. On one of our last days, I became more courageous and I swam out further into it than I ever had before. I felt like being a little dangerous and wanted to see how far out I could swim without scaring me out of my wits. When I reached the farthest reaches, well beyond other swimmers, I began treading in the water, floating around, and enjoying one of my last days of vacation. I was probably a good twenty yards away from the nearest swimmer. The sun was high in the sky and warm on my face and I felt great...

Until I noticed something odd. As I looked down the entire beach front, everyone was getting out of the water. I immediately wondered what was going on. As I was treading water, I heard words which I will never forget. The lifeguard shouted through his megaphone, "Everyone out of the water; everyone out of the water; SHARKS! SHARKS!" I had never heard more frightening words. I turned around and sure enough, swimming out near a tanker further out were about a dozen fins. Immediately, I swam toward the shore as fast as I could. There was only one problem—all I could think about was all of those shark attack stories I had read. I knew everything about sharks. I knew how they attacked, who they attacked, and when they attacked. At that very moment, my single thought was this—a shark's favorite meal were adventurous boys from Illinois! I kept pumping my arms; kicking my legs; and flaying away as fast as I could in that cool salt water. Finally, without a scratch on me, I crawled up onto shore. Just then, standing above me was the lifeguard and into his megaphone he yelled, "False alarm. Just dolphins." After that, I decided it was best just to make sandcastles and didn't go swimming the rest of that vacation. Here is a truth I learned that day—sometimes, things aren't what they seem.

And sometimes people aren't what they seem. This takes us to our next point about who believers are. Typically, believers want to have it their way; they want to lead two different lives. This was exactly what I was doing when I first became a Christian during my freshman year in college. Every now and then, I would hang out with my Christian friends, pretending to be a changed person, but then later that night I would end up in bed with my girlfriend. I kept her a secret from everyone, and she and I would have our rendezvous' usually after midnight. I was not who I portrayed myself to be. I was someone entirely different and no one knew.

Believers try to have their cake and eat it too; they try to see if they can pull off living the new and old life at the same time. But it never works. Again, in the book of Revelation, in his words to the church of Laodicea, Jesus shares with us the description of one who has been a dedicated believer too long: "I know you inside and out, and find little to my liking. You're not cold, you're not hot—far better to be either cold or hot! You're stale. You're stagnant. You make me want to vomit. You brag, 'I'm rich, I've got it made, I need nothing from anyone,' oblivious that in fact you're a pitiful, blind beggar, threadbare and homeless." (Revelation 3:15-17, The Message)

Ouch! That's what I love about the Bible, it always tells it like it is. Believers are neither this or that; they try to be all things. Again, this was Judas: he tried to remain friends with those who hated Jesus and those who were also his closest confidants—the disciples. He tried to be spiritual and carnal at the same time. In the same day, Judas most likely would have lunch with the Pharisees and then go have dinner with Jesus and the disciples. Judas was sitting there nodding in agreement with Jesus when he was on the mountain teaching the throngs of people, and then later that evening nodding again, but this time, with his friends from previous days. Most of the time, Judas was doing his own thing and when it was convenient, he would do the Jesus' thing. There was little consistency in his life and perhaps at times, he would see the truth in Jesus' words, but in the next moment, he was off doing his own thing, finding his own way in life. Simply put, Judas was a fraud and this type of living cost him his life, literally hanging on the limb of a tree when he took his own life.

Going back to our theological primer in an earlier chapter, in this world there are two kingdoms vying with one another. This is a simple fact. Again, as Bob Dylan wrote, you are either in one camp or in the other. This is not a both/and question; it is an either/or one. Either you are with Jesus, or you are not with Jesus. These are his own words. You cannot sit on the fence. Jesus emphatically joins the question by saying: "Whoever is not with me is against me, and whoever does not gather with me scatters." (Matthew 12:30) Every day you get up you have to decide, am I with Jesus or not?

If you think about it, it was always a misnomer to call Judas a disciple or follower of Jesus. Perhaps for a time he was, a very brief time, but like the seed that fell on stony ground Judas sprouted up, but only for a brief moment (Matthew 13:1-23). This is exactly why it is so very important to continually move deeper with Jesus. Every day we need to let him further into our lives, to let him invade every inch of our being, let him control each and every matter. And this is why this is so important—all of this is for our benefit any way. I have learned in my life so well that when I stay close to him, everything is good, no matter what the situation or circumstance. This is why I am certain that when he continues to pull me back, when I begin to stray from him, it's for my good, not his. It's for me, first and foremost, and it is because of this tremendous concern that he has for me that he will never let me go.

ME, ME, ME

The tragedy of life and of the world is not that men do not know God; the tragedy is that, knowing Him, they still insist on going their own way.

William Barclay

My soul is impatient with itself, as with a bothersome child; its restlessness keeps growing and is forever the same. Everything interests me, but nothing holds me.

Fernando Pessoa

It is easy, when you are young, to believe that what you desire is no less than what you deserve, to assume that if you want something badly enough, it is your God-given right to have it.

Jon Krakauer

Another aspect is the reality that believers typically are self-centered, rather than God-centered in the way they live their life. This was especially my struggle in my early years of faith: I wanted it my way (and sometimes continues to be so). I thought that after giving my life to God, I could just continue living the way I had before and not much would need to change. At the heart of it, people are selfish and this is because we live in a fallen world and put simply, because we our sinners. It's a very hard thing to give our lives over to someone and trust that they have our best intentions for us. Selfishness is at the root of human sin and God begins to address it right off the bat when we move into a relationship with him. Those who have recently come to faith face this challenge squarely, because it is something God wishes to render obsolete in us right from the start.

Most people usually have this on their minds at most times—me, me, me. Because God understands that to be disconnected from him is dangerous, he pushes us to be focused on him first. He is our life and without him, we are nothing. The Heidelberg Catechism puts it in a way which is perhaps the most eloquent way of professing this truth:

Question 1. What is thy only comfort in life and death?

> Answer: That I with body and soul, both in life and death, am not my own, but belong unto my faithful Saviour Jesus Christ; who, with his precious blood, has fully satisfied for all my sins, and delivered me from all the power of the devil; and so preserves me that without the will of my heavenly Father, not a hair can fall from my head; yea, that all things must be subservient to my salvation, and therefore, by his Holy Spirit, He also assures me of eternal life, and makes me sincerely willing and ready, henceforth, to live unto him.

Now, that is beautiful. But the danger lies in the question, what if I give up all my rights, all of my control, what will he do with my life then? What will it cost me? How can I trust a God I can't even see? How can I trust anyone, when no one has ever been constant for me? These are all the questions that fumble around in the mind of a believer. Following Jesus is a dangerous thing and challenging at times, and it takes tremendous risk. To give myself over to another, who wants to do that? I have to look after myself. If I don't, who will? These are the statements that the world offers to us every day and they are melded into our minds. With this, when we begin to follow God, we naturally do it half-heartedly. We don't give it our all. We wait and see how things will turn out. This is precisely what Judas did. He was waiting to see how things were going to turn out and when it looked as if everything was falling apart, he went and made an appointment with the chief priest to see if a deal could be made. Jesus tells us though that this is no way to live. Over and over, he challenges us that to live for him, we must do it unselfishly. The problem is that nowhere in the world will we find a model in which to live like this. This is a new thing and a new way of living. Innately, to live such a life goes against our very nature and to do so requires tremendous trust and a risk like no other. What's the payout? Jesus says, everything you have always wanted.

How does one not begin to live for themselves? Just like the risk involved, it is a task like no other. By first putting our focus on God and then, on others, is a painful process. It's like having your heart ripped out and it can feel as if you are dying until you get that new one in its place. This is the difficult challenge, because we are all taught at some level that we can only trust ourselves. But the way of Jesus is a new one. We are taught that to rely on another is foolishness; he asserts that to give is better than receiving (Acts 20:35). Now that is crazy! Overtime, however, we must begin to relinquish ourselves and genuinely give if we desire to truly grow. This is the main approach of growth. In those times in my life as I look back, I grew the most when I was giving myself to someone else and making genuine sacrifices. It can be tiring and excruciating, but in the end it is the right thing. With respect to this, I think of something that A.W. Tozer wrote:

> The labor of self-love is a heavy one indeed. Think for yourself whether much of your sorrow has not arisen from someone speaking slightingly of you. As along as you set yourself up as a little god to which you must be loyal, how can you hope to find inward peace?

Again, to live a life that is only focussed on myself is difficult, challenging and actually limits me in the end. In each of our lives, we need to find that place, where at the end of the day we learn to put into practice that we don't just look out for ourselves, we look out for each person that God has placed around us. It really is true—it is so much better to give than to receive—that when we take our gaze off ourselves and onto others is actually liberating.

THE COMPANY WE KEEP

Tell me what company you keep, and I will tell you what you are.
Cervantes
The hardest thing in life is to know which bridge to cross and which to burn.
David Russell

A final sign that a person may be just a believer is when one looks at their friendships. As mentioned earlier, God made us for others, and others are made for our good as well. It's a reciprocal relationship. This is the epitome of what it means to be the body of Christ—the powerful influence of good friendships. Believers, however, often shun friendships with those who share in their faith. Often, because their life is so crazy and out of whack, it's difficult and uncomfortable for them to hang out and befriend those who have a relationship with God. I knew this firsthand. Early on when I became a Christian, I did not enjoy being around those who shared my new-found faith, because my conscience was always telling me things were not quite right in my life. To be with other Christians in some sense seemed to reveal to me how I was really living—that there were significant parts of my life that were misaligned. Therefore, there was a time in my life when I had few friends who had a relationship with God. Ironically, for me, my closest friends were actually adverse to Christianity, and whenever we got in discussions about faith or similar topics, they would let me know in no uncertain terms how they felt about my faith. Eventually, I dropped the topic altogether.

At that time, I was a follower, but not really a follower of Jesus. My friends influenced my beliefs and actions more than I did theirs. Here are some questions to ask yourself if you might be in this stage of faith—1) who are you impacting in your life, and 2) who influences or mentors you? Overall, are your friendships genuinely healthy and moving you forward emotionally and spiritually? And if some of those friendships are not healthy, are your friends influencing you in negative ways? Do you gravitate toward their way of life in harmful ways? If most of your friendships are negatively influencing your life, you probably need some new friends.

This is always a difficult topic to talk about because sometimes friendships such as these have been a part of our lives for a long time, perhaps even since childhood. At this point in my own life, this was a very difficult decision that I had to make. I had had a friend of many years, but when we were together, it was really David who directed my life. I can clearly remember one day in which God said to me, *It is David or it is Me.* God knew that I could never become the person I was supposed to be if David had this much influence in my life. But with this, David was no devil or some awful person; he was kind and generous and had brought a lot of good things into my life. God loved David, but he also knew that there were aspects in which he was holding me back with my relationship with him, and if I was going to move in the right direction, I would have to give up that friendship, because in many ways it was very unhealthy. As one example, David was adamantly an atheist and if ever a topic about faith came up, he quickly and angrily squelched it. The reality of it was that when I was around him, I could never really be myself. And isn't that the prerequisite of a good friendship—you can always be yourself? As St. Augustine wrote:

> Bad company is like a nail driven into a post, which, after the first or second blow, may be drawn out with little difficulty; but being once driven up to the head, the pincers cannot take hold to draw it out, but which can only be done by the destruction of the wood.

Of course, we can't always alienate our lives from those who don't share our faith; Jesus never isolated himself from those who were foreign to his words and ways. But his model is our model—his most intimate of relationships were with those who knew him. We do have to be careful with whom we share our lives. As the famous Proverb states, "Above all else, guard your heart for it is the wellspring of life." (4:23) Our most intimate of relationships most likely will be with those who share this unique and beautiful relationship that we have with Jesus. When we want to open up and share what is going on in our lives with our relationship with God, these will be people who know what we are talking about. For others, who do not share in this, they will simply think we are speaking a foreign language, and therefore, this is why we really need to assess our friendships to see how healthy or unhealthy they are.

THE DANGER IN BELIEVING IN GOD

The longer we analyze the current ways of operating, the further we fend off that awesome day when we will have to change something. Analysis thus becomes a defensive maneuver to avoid making fundamental change.

Michael Hammer and Steven Stanton

So many Christians think that because they believe in the right God, they are automatically good and have a one-way ticket to everlasting life. Dare I say it, but I suspect this is their main reason for believing. I've heard so many 'believers' say, "Well, since there is no way of being sure whether there is a God or not, it's better to believe in God than not, because that way, if you're wrong it doesn't matter and if you're right you get everlasting life." Win:win.

Ricky Gervais

A great many people think they are thinking when they are merely rearranging their prejudices.

William James

The Scriptures tell us a plain truth: "Believe in the Lord Jesus and you will be saved." (Acts 16:31) The first step of faith is pretty easy and self-explanatory. At the same time, it is only the first step. Believe it or not, it can be dangerous to "just" believe in God. One needs to grow, move on, confront life and enter into a deeper relationship with him. Believers, in the end, only stagnate. Satan, in purest form, *believes* in Jesus; he knows who Jesus is, knows what he is all about—even met him face-to-face a few times. The great difference is that he does not give Jesus his allegiance; he doesn't offer Him his life and his worship. With that, there is a great chasm. This is often where the believer can stand.

Are you just a believer? How would you know if you were? We can find a whole lot of "just believers" in the Bible: from Esau to Saul to Ananias and Sapphira. These are perfect examples of those who simply believed in God, but didn't take it much farther than that. Again, in the New Testament, we find the perfect example and that is through Judas. By looking at his life, we can discover how not to be a follower of Jesus. Judas had little love and little dedication to Jesus. He wanted life his way. He wanted to hide what was really going on in his life. He lived a life of compromise. In living this way, tragically, he ended his own life with tremendous regret.

You have heard this before: it does not matter how you begin a race; the importance lies in how you finish. This is the danger that we face if we don't take our relationship with God and move it further. It is a simple truth spoken throughout the Bible—God wants all or nothing. This is why it so crucial that when you give your life to God that you don't stop there. The consequences are just too great. On that day of believing, the journey has just begun and we cannot forget that the great commission that Jesus challenged was to make followers—to make disciples (not believers) of all nations and tongues (Matthew 28: 16-20).

So with respect to this, there is an element in which our relationship with God is willed. Listen carefully to what St. Augustine said about this: "One can say: 'I will, but my body does not obey me;' but not: 'My will does not obey me.'" In our life, we are continuously offered choices and in some respects "our will" is the chief character. It is no different than when we start a relationship with God—we make it happen with *his* help. Just as we had to make that decision to follow him, whether it was one Thursday night at a Bible study or at some tent revival, it is us who says yes. God never forces us to believe in him—He will never say this yes for us. I like the image and word that the Scripture offers; it says that God woos us (Isaiah 43:1-7). It shows him as being patient, and placing his affection in the midst of our lives. Like a young man who is trying to win the affection of a woman, God gently and carefully moves into our lives. He wants to be known and to have the responsibility of loving and caring for us. But again, he will never make the decision for us. He never forces himself into our lives. We must make the decision to love him back. Every day we must say yes to him. Yes to believing, yes to giving our lives to him, yes to obeying, yes to friendship. Every day we must learn how to say yes to him.

HOW A TRIP TO TORONTO CAN CHANGE YOUR LIFE

I believe in the Kingdom Come/Then all the colors will bleed into one/Bleed into one/But yes I'm still running/But I still haven't found what I'm looking for. U2

The deepest proof for God's existence, apart from history, is just life itself. God has created man in his image, and men cannot elude the implications of this fact. Everywhere their identity pursues them. Ultimately, there is no escape. Clark Pinnock

Life's sloppy. You think you know how tomorrow is going to be, you've made your plans, everything is set in place, and then the unimaginable happens. Life catches you by surprise. It always does. But there's good mixed in with the bad. It's there. You just have to recognize it. Susan Beth Pfeffer

I had my own experience in which I had lived as a believer too long. I was a junior in college and I was definitely living two lives. I was going to church, and occasionally living out my beliefs; I even went on a mission trip during that time. I had such great motives. The problem was —it was just so difficult to get my actions to follow. You see, I was also another person. When one has an impersonal relationship with God, they inevitably do not know themselves or their importance in life. They will go where the wind blows. Even with all of my confidence on the outside, internally I was a mess. I played a good game; I knew how to impress; I knew how to wear the mask. But I was also the person who had dark secrets hiding just under the surface.

At the core, at that time in my life, God was not my security; relationships with women were. During that school year, I was in a handful of different relationships. Most of them were shallow. Most of them were based on what I could get out of them. Just like me, these women were just out for a good time. At this point in my life, there was one woman I had had my eye on for a long time. To this day, I remember her name; it was Julia.

Julia was my kind of woman. She was artsy; she was European (literally) and bohemian; she had a way about her—elegant and angular. The way she wore her hair; the way her clothes hung off her body; the way she spoke with her Italian accent—it all mesmerized me. Julia was in a class that we shared together, and overtime we became friends, and I kept my infatuation for her hidden. The college where we attended had a two-week break during January and most students got out of the city and ventured off to other areas of the country. Over coffee at the Harrison Diner one day, Julia mentioned that she was going to Toronto over break and she wondered if I would like to go with her. I was pleasantly ecstatic. Of course, I would, and so we began making plans.

In all of my days, I will never forget that drive to Toronto. I love driving early in the morning, getting up at 3 a.m., having a cup of coffee in hand, and driving through the early dawn. It was something I grew up with as a kid; as a family, we always started our vacations just before sunrise and it's always stuck with me. Before daybreak, I picked up Julia at her apartment and we headed out on I-94, heading east toward Canada. We were cruising along, chit-chatting and had the music turned up. It was a very cold January night and when we reached just across the Michigan border, it began sleeting. I slowed the car down a bit, but drove on. Just past Kalamazoo, I thought I heard something pop, but I just kept on driving. At that section of the highway, it was three lanes and I was driving in the middle lane. There was a semi-truck behind me, one in front, one to my right, and one to my left. I was surrounded by all of these semi-trucks and we sped down the road at seventy miles per hour. Unbeknownst to me, my tire had blown. Unbeknownst to me, there was ice an inch thick on the road. Unbeknownst to me, the car was about to slide out of control.

I was driving nervous, both hands on the wheel, knuckles white.

Stupidly, I sped up to about eighty and moved into the right lane of the highway. I wanted to get to that far right lane as quick as I could, because in my gut I knew something wasn't right. However, as I made the lane change, my 1977 Chevy Caprice Classic skidded aimlessly toward a guardrail, just missing an eighteen-wheeler. Julia screamed and I tried to keep the car under control. Thankfully, no cars (or semis) hit us, but we did hit the guardrail in dramatic fashion. Julia was hysterical and I was rattled by the circumstance as well. I got out of the car and looked over the damage that actually wasn't that bad (they just don't make cars like that anymore). As I ventured toward the back of the car I saw that my rear passenger tire was in shreds. I got out the jack and began replacing the blown wheel. It was freezing out and like a lot of forgetful 20-year-olds, I hadn't packed very well and I didn't have a winter coat. It was January—Julia was sitting in the car crying and traffic was whizzing by me as I attempted to change the tire.

After about forty-five minutes later, we were driving again, Julia was still upset, and so I asked her if she wanted to get in the backseat and go to sleep. Not a half an hour later, right outside of Jackson, I was driving along in the early morning, and just out of nowhere the car did a 360° spin right in the middle of the highway. That's how icy it was. Thankfully, no cars were in front or in back of me. I was now shaking. I got out of the car and literally slipped to the ground because now there was a thick layer of ice on the grass and road. I was trembling and was audibly thanking God for protecting us. I climbed back into the front seat and Julia was shaking the sleep off, rubbing her eyes, and asked if everything was okay. I lied. I said things were fine. I also added that I thought it would be best if we pulled over for a while until all of the ice melted.

At this moment in time, God was talking to me. He was trying to get my attention. I knew and he knew that it was not best for me to be on this trip with this attractive Italian woman. It was just another attempt of me running away from what I really needed to face. Right there, I should've turned around and gone back home, but I didn't. God was trying to get my attention and I ignored him. Julia and I decided to stay in Jackson that night at some crummy motel. Nothing happened as we slept next to one another—but you know what, I wanted it to and that was all that mattered. I was running as hard as I could away from God no different than Jonah.

We finally got to Toronto and I met Julia's friends and our time together was filled with a lot of drinking. The first day we were there, three of the guys brewed their own beer and we drank a lot of it. Julia was originally from Lithuania and the next night we ended up going to a Lithuanian festival. At first, I was having a great time; I was drinking a little; I was talking to a lot of different people. But deep down, I was terribly sad. I looked around at the people and everything seemed so depressing to me. The whole situation was depressing. Slowly, but surely, I was realizing how depressing my life was. I was running away from God and it was finally catching up with me. We sat down to eat and not shortly after we were seated, I heard God speak to me more clearly than maybe I ever have before. In my mind, I heard two simple words: Go home. That was all that I heard, but it was enough. It was a voice that was firm; it was a voice that was serious. God was trying to get my attention and I knew those words were for me. I got up out of my chair went over to Julia and told her I was heading home. She commented that she would see me when she got home and asked me if I knew the way back to her friend's apartment. I explained to her that I was actually heading back home to Chicago and just like that, I was out the door.

Herbert Agar has said, "The truth which makes men free is for the most part the truth which men prefer not to hear." This was exactly where I was at in my life. On that journey home, it was as if Jesus was literally sitting in the car seat next to me and we drove home silent, not a word being said between the two of us. On the way back to Chicago, I was almost involved in another car accident, driving through a snowstorm, and again, I got out of the car shaking at the knees. It was confirmed, I knew God was trying to drive home a point. He was attempting to tell me something rather simple: *Kelly, you must give me all of yourself. Not just the crumbs. If you want to be with me, you must live all of your life for me. Now, it's up to you.*

Now, it's up to you. Those words pierced me because that was the full truth. That night as I drove into the city, I parked my car outside my apartment and just listened to the silence in the cold. That night just sitting there, I did my very best at relinquishing all of these unruly desires and the pursuits of unhealthy relationships. At that interval in my life, it was the most out of control it had ever been. I was frantic for love, but for the wrong kind. Even though I could not put it into words at that time, that night I tried to put Jesus at the center. That January night, sitting cold in my Chevy Caprice Classic on Oak Park Avenue, for the first time I became a follower of Jesus, his follower, his disciple, his servant. At that moment, I tried to fall in love with him and with no other. I tried to really follow him for the first time.

> Here's what I want you to do: Buy your gold from me, gold that's been through the refiner's fire. Then you'll be rich. Buy your clothes from me, clothes designed in Heaven. You've gone around half-naked long enough. And buy medicine for your eyes from me so you can see, really see. The people I love, I call to account—prod and correct and guide so that they'll live at their best. Up on your feet, then! About face! Run after God! Look at me. I stand at the door. I knock. If you hear me call and open the door, I'll come right in and sit down to supper with you. (Revelation 3:18-20, The Message)

ARE YOU STUCK IN YOUR FAITH?

In summary of this section, the person who is just a believer is someone who believes in God, but in reality, it is they who run and direct their lives. They probably attend church very irregularly. They usually are not involved at their church in any way. They rarely, if ever, read the Bible or pray (perhaps only over a meal or because a crisis in their life has occurred). If you were to really ask them what they believe, they really wouldn't be sure why they believe in God at all. So, are you a believer? Here might be some tale-tale signs:

- Do you find that God is distant even though you gave your life to him years ago?
- Who runs your life? You, God or something else? What is first for you: people, material things or God? Look at where you spend your time—where is your devotion? What is most important to you?
- Do you have convictions or do you free wheel it when it comes to what is right or wrong? Most of the time, what do you do when your conscience speaks to you—change your path or ignore that voice?
- Do you have a hard time talking about God? Can you pray out loud? Is that because of shyness or is it really because God just isn't very real to you and prayer itself is uncomfortable?
- Do others know that you are a Christian (e.g., at work, your school, your friends, etc.)? Is this common knowledge or do you usually keep that a secret from others?
- What is your commitment level? To others? To church? How involved are you? Is church a common occurrence or do you often find yourself finding an excuse early Sunday morning of why you shouldn't go?

- Do others know the real you? How good are you at faking it? Do you have some significant problems that you probably should face?
- Who are your real friends? With your closest relationships, how many of those friendships are centered on Jesus and you both learning about his life? For those friendships in which the other person is not a Christian—who influences who—does that other person influence you more than the other way around?
- Is there something that stands in your way in following God and making him number one in your life? A relationship? Your work? Some kind of sin that is always standing in your way?
- Is Jesus simply your Savior, but not the Lord or leader of your life?

Part Three
Following Too Hard After God

THE PERFECT SERVANT - PETER

This is a fictitious short story written about a moment in the life of Peter from the perspective of one of the twelve disciples, Thaddaeus. It is a picture of what Peter was like before he learned about grace and truly knowing what Jesus was all about.

To be honest, we were all getting sick and tired of him. I think even Jesus was fed up, because every now and then Jesus would just let into him like I never had seen before. Jesus was very serious in these times and he made sure that you understood that he wasn't joking. He did this all too often with Peter.

I want to be honest about this—for the most part, you just never really want to be around Peter. He has to do it his way and there is always no other way with him. To a word, he is demanding. That was the thing that puzzled us all so much, because on the one hand, Jesus could be so hard on Peter, but then at the other, Peter was always at his side and seemed to be his favorite. Often, this perplexed us. I remember one time in particular when Jesus had left us for a few hours and ventured off to be by himself—Peter just went crazy, telling us all what to do. He chided almost every single one of us, but specifically both Thomas and Bartholomew really got it that day. He went on and on about how he was disgusted with their subtle criticisms of where we were going and how we were spending our time. He lost it, ranted, raved, and cursed them as his face got red. We all just stood there, white-faced and our mouth's open, amazed at what we were seeing and hearing. We couldn't believe the words that were coming out of his mouth. This was when I began keeping my distance from him. Peter could be passionate, but he could also be dangerous. He seemed only to hurt those around him with his words and actions.

The incident that really pushed everyone over the edge was just yesterday. After this, out of all eleven of us, I don't think Peter has one friend; maybe his brother Andrew, but that is just because they are brothers. Granted, it was late and we were hungry and most of us were a bit edgy, because we knew that something was about to happen. I still cannot understand how he could say such words, especially because of all that we had gone through in these last years as brothers. Jesus was trying to get it into our heads that by going to Jerusalem something was going to change, something dramatic was going to occur. Admittedly, we were all a bit afraid, but Peter said some things which I am not sure any of us will forget. That was no way to talk to someone. To be honest, I was a bit angry that Jesus didn't confront him on his attitude toward us.

It wasn't what Peter said so much as how he said it. He spoke with venom. As Jesus was telling us in his own way that there would be challenges ahead for us as we went to the city, Peter in his loud and boisterous way, spit into the air his words, "Jesus, these, these, may forget about you, but I will never!" Angrily, he was pointing his finger, sweeping it across us all. Again, he shouted, "These, Rabbi, may forsake you, but not me!" After that, I never trusted Peter. Maybe he had more zeal than all of us, but something is just not right about that man. I can't put my finger on it, but I wouldn't be surprised if things end badly with him. His passion is strong, but his gentleness is none. Nothing good can happen to a man like that. There is only one hope for him; Jesus is going to have to do something dramatic to change him.

MAKING IT WORSE

It was not dogma that moved the world, but life. W. M. Ramsay

A.W. Tozer, one of the most gifted Christian authors, entitled his most famous work *Following Hard After God*. It's a great title. It is one of my favorite books and I can remember reading it some years ago. The book spoke very plainly about having a relationship with God, but in a gentle and beneficial way. It broke me down, and yet it lifted me up. The best writing is remarkable; it not only speaks eloquently, but in an obvious way cuts to the heart with its nouns, verbs and prepositional phrases. However, in thinking about that title today in relation to this chapter, strangely enough, one can also follow too hard after God. A person can miss the point entirely when they follow Him with nothing more than a bunch of zeal.

When one desires to make more of their relationship with God, they make this remarkable decision to no longer just being a believer, but they now want to be his servant. They want God not just to be their Savior, but they invite him to be the Leader in their lives as well. They want to truly attempt to live for him and for him only. And let's be clear —this transformation from believer to a servant is a natural and necessary one. Following hard after God is a good thing and can be good for us, but only up to a point. Letting our lives flow through what God desires for us is right and good. Making those necessary changes in which we move from seeing Jesus not just as Savior, but as our Lord is good, really good, and yet it's not enough. The journey does not end here.

Just as it can be dangerous to stay a believer too long, the same goes for being a servant of Jesus. This may seem like an odd statement. On the one hand, the servant is beginning to get it right. All those aspects in which they move from "just believing" to truly obeying is good stuff. Being passionate about ones faith, learning to throw off the hindrances of sin, finding friendships that build one up rather than tear one down, being solid in one's understandings and beliefs—all of these are wise decisions, which lead to greater depth to one's relationship with God. But again, as the infamous brother-sister duo of the 1970's The Carpenter's remind us, *We've only just begun.* Let's say it one more time—becoming a Christian takes a lifetime. In thinking about all of this, this isn't what we want though—we don't want it to take that long. We want it now. We think it's better if it's easier, faster. We want the goodies right from the start. But deep down, we also know that anything good never comes this way. The best things need to be learned, whether that is learning how to play the guitar, training to run a marathon or simply becoming an extraordinary father, brother, mother, sister or friend.

But let's get back to all this "servant stuff," because we really can learn a lot by looking at the life of Peter. He is the servant of all servants. Go look at the life of Peter in the New Testament books of Matthew, Mark, Luke and John. In the gospels, he's passionate, conceited, arrogant, single-minded, legalistic, cruel, selfish, focused, foolish, long-winded, big-on-himself, and also dedicated to Jesus big time. Can you see the hypocrisy and duplicity? Can you see the problem? On the one hand, he had it right (put Jesus Number One in your life) and on the other he had it all wrong (hot-headed and hypocritical). Peter was two people—the passionate follower and the loose cannon. The central problem was that his passions were misguided. Here's the key, they were based on rules and not relationship. It just wasn't in his heart—literally. All of this stuff came from what he knew—to know God meant to obey the rules, follow the instructions to the letter, to know the manual inside and out. This was the mode of operation found exclusively in the Old Testament and the kind of stuff that the Israelites got hung up on. Peter was just continuing the cycle.

It all began really well with Jesus when he met him fishing; but then

Peter made it worse. He became a terror—mean-spirited, angry and entirely missed the point. He was becoming all that he wasn't supposed to be. Let's just give a few descriptors to who Peter was becoming: stern and hollow; had to follow all the rules at all costs; a mile wide, but an inch deep; trying to be perfectly obedient; working only through his own strength; he thought he had all the answers. That's just naming a few. Jesus, however, was going to teach him something new. Jesus was going to move Peter to a place where he was supposed to be—into friendship with his Creator. When he gets to that place, compare that same guy in the rest of the New Testament, beyond the gospels. He is a totally different person in those other books, in particular through his own two letters (I and II Peter) we see this clearly. He's slow with his words; he's generous; he's kind and patient; he puts others before himself; he's got love by the horns. Peter finally became Jesus' friend and it took a miracle unlike any other that Jesus had performed, and it happened with just a short conversation. We'll get to that story later on.

Brennan Manning in his book A Glimpse of Jesus relates this story. He remarks that a well-intentioned friend offered a eulogy to someone recently deceased: "John was a wonderful Christian. He never missed church, was married only once, and never told a dirty joke." But is that what a Christian's main goal in life is to be—gets to church on time and never says a cuss word? This is what can so easily happen when one ventures on with Jesus. Come on, let's admit it; it's so much easier to follow a bunch of rules rather than be in a relationship with the One who is more amazing than we can imagine. Boxing ourselves in with a bunch of laws, conventions and systems seems like the most sensible way. It's easier that way. But it's not the best way.

And just as you can stay a believer too long, it can be said the same for the servant. There is a danger in being "just" a servant. Think of the Pharisees. In some ways, Peter was acting just like them. First, they followed a bunch of rules and regulations for themselves, and then, in the end, put all that junk on others. This was exactly where Peter was going in his own life, and Jesus had to stop him and stop him quick. You might remember that Jesus had made Peter the go-to-guy, referring to him as the Rock (Matthew 16:18) and if he was going to lead his church in this manner—Peter could have really messed everything up. If Peter had had his way, being a Christian would have become some warped version of what Jesus intended—it would have boiled down to just following a bunch of rules. Do this; don't' do that. In this, Jesus had to drive home his point in a very striking and painful way to Peter. You might even remember how Jesus made that point with Peter; he used a rooster and a teenage girl to teach Peter a lesson or two. After that incident, that following week for Peter was a very long one. Life was put on hold and Peter had no idea where he stood. It was a terribly humbling experience. But in the end, he learned something that he just could not understand in the previous three years of knowing Jesus. During those years, Peter kept getting it wrong. Now all of that was about to change. Sooner or later, he would realize that being a friend to Jesus was even better than being his servant.

KNOWING IT ALL

It is the greatest truth of our age: Information is not knowledge. Caleb Carr

When you are too sure about God and faith, you are sure of something other than God: of dogma, of the church, of a particular interpretation of the Bible. But God cannot be pigeonholed. We must press toward certainty, but be suspicious when it comes too glibly. Stan Wiersma

And here is the main problem with basing your faith on obeying a bunch of rules. Once you get it down, once you become really adept at basing your relationship with God on making sure you you are doing everything just right—it's real easy to become what I call a know-it-all. Have you ever met a know-it-all? This is a person who when you are in a room talking and you ask a question, this person comes out of nowhere and gives you the answer uninvited. This is the person who, in any kind of discussion, they never let up and will make sure they have the last word. This is the know-it-all:

- The best books to read—*where do I start?*
- The reason for poverty—*let me give you the real answer.*
- How to make a proper omelet—*let me show you how.*
- The very best political candidate—*let me tell you a thing or two.*
- How to live a righteous life—*I've got that one down.*

Of course, there are degrees to this type of person; some people are worse than others. And of course, there are those who are genuinely knowledgeable, but there is distinction between that type of person and the know-it-all. Usually that distinction is that for the know-it-all, there is an arrogance or pride mixed into the batter. There is a way in which they use their knowledge as a weapon or in a manner in which they get to shine and be the center of attention.

Very easily, one can turn into this person once one has been a Christian for some time. Remember, just believing in God is simply mental assent and it is easy to use knowledge as the device in which one grows their relationship with God. Knowledge then becomes the end pursuit. The end game then can become this: having a greater understanding of doctrine, knowing the biblical premise behind baptism, knowing the prophetic literature of the Old Testament inside and out, etc.—this is what makes you a Christian. Now, nothing is wrong with any of these kinds of pursuits, but it boils down to the motivation behind that learning. Usually, we pursue knowledge for two reasons: for understanding or for power. The student who enters medical school can learn about disease and the interaction with the human body to help others or they can study and log in all of those hours simply for more money or to wield their influence over others. Each aspect of knowledge is like this: I have met people who learn about world history, languages, computers, fashion, engineering, literature, mechanics, parenting, the tax code, and even the Bible, not for the joy of learning and growing, but simply to be able to wield that knowledge over others. In the end though, this pursuit for knowledge becomes a machine to impress or control.

This is exactly why this period in the Christian life can be so dangerous. All that we know at this point about God in some sense is just knowledge and information. This is the Peter that we read about in the gospels. Read one of them and see how much he knows and how often Jesus challenges him on what he knows. Over and over, he is telling Peter, "No, it's not quite that way…let me explain it this way to you." Do you remember the scene in which Jesus actually calls Peter the devil? This is Jesus challenging him as the know-it-all. He basically tells Peter to shut up. That's how bad Peter was getting in his arrogance. (Matthew 16:23)

This is what Jesus saw in Peter—he was becoming very much like the Pharisees, the teachers of the law with whom he always had the harshest words. The Pharisees were the crème of the crop when it came to being know-it-alls. This importance of knowledge over relationship with God is the chief complaint Jesus has against them. The Pharisees were careful students of the Jewish law, and in fact, in Jesus' eyes—too careful. They had the Scriptures memorized backward and forwards; they definitively knew what was right and what was wrong. In this pursuit of information, they even had come up with some of their own rules! But they missed the point entirely. In contrast, St. Augustine was so audacious with this issue that he wrote that "God is best known in not knowing him." What Augustine was attempting to say was that pursuing just knowledge in the end could get in the way of genuinely understanding who God is.

And so with that, in the end the Pharisees began to misuse the dogma they studied. This is the tremendous pitfall of the one who bases their entire experience with God simply on attaining knowledge about him—they will eventually miss the major points like grace, forgiveness, and freedom in Christ. These are things they have never experienced personally, and therefore, these points of importance don't connect with them internally. Their knowledge is merely based on rote learning which is flat and impersonal. This person might be able to talk at length about grace and other such theological fundamentals, but genuinely experiencing them is distant and missed. This is why Jesus called them "blind guides." (Matthew 23:16) If a person has the essentials of faith wrong, they will obviously begin teaching others these ungrounded presumptions, which will cause further harm. Look at all the unsettling stuff that gets propagated in the church today.

- You shouldn't go to "rock" concerts.
- So and so is the best preacher and you should only listen to him.
- You have to read this version of the Bible.
- Those who have cancer or relationships problems (or any other problem) just don't have enough faith.
- That woman should not have her hair cut so short (or that guy so long)!
- You have to be baptized in this exact and precise way.

- To be a real Christian, you have to attend our church.

Obviously some rules are actually right and good, but sometimes rules can turn into something that becomes a prerequisite to having a relationship with God. However, the truth is that some of these standards that we put on ourselves and others have little to do with having a relationship with God at all.

And here might be the most important point—as Christians we have the freedom to NOT know everything. In no way shape or form do we have to know it all. All of life is complex and there are mysteries to which we may never know. Events will occur in our lives that will leave us haunted by these experiences and not until we see God face-to-face will we understand. As the Bible says, "Now we see but a poor reflection as in a mirror; then we shall see face to face. Now I know in part; then I shall know fully, even as I am fully known." (1 Corinthians 13:12) The world and universe is vast and to expect to have it all down and understood is impossible. There are problems we may face which simply do not have clear and cut answers. When we are presented with a difficult question or problem, it can be relieving to just say these simple words, "I do not know." There can be a blessing in not knowing it all—it leaves us room to continue to explore. The theologian Clark Pinnock (as an aside, with his writings, he was very instrumental in our understanding about the infallibility of the Bible) says words which we would be well-advised to think about in relationship to our own lives when we have misgivings with our faith:

> I know what it is to doubt and question. And I suspect
> that every Christian who takes the time to think seriously
> about his faith does so too.

I think these are good words for us to remember. We need to always remember that we don't have to always know it all.

THE MOST IMPORTANT QUESTION: DOES JESUS KNOW ME?

Later I would discover, very gradually, that that is one of the chief characteristics of love: it asks for everything. Not just for a little bit or for a whole lot, but for everything. And unless one is challenged to give everything, one is not really in love. Mike Mason

Let me now say it a third time—becoming a servant to Jesus is important and necessary, but there are also pitfalls. It is clear that we can have faith in God, but then miss the point entirely. At one point in the gospels, Jesus speaks some really daunting and ear-catching words. Let me set the scene. First, he said that there will come a day when standing before him at the judgment there will some who will say that they a lot of great things in his name. They will tell him they've cast out a bunch of demons, healed a bunch of people, led multitudes to himself, even wrote Christian books—basically did all these great works for God. They'll be exclaiming, look at what I did Jesus, aren't you proud of me! However, he will simply come back and state these haunting words, "I never knew you." (Matthew 7:21-23) Whoah! Once again, it's Jesus turning things on its head—addressing something from a different angle and exposing a truth we never saw. What we think is true, may not necessarily be the case. With this story, we see that there will be a lot of people who are doing incredible things for God, but in the end, these folks will turn out to be essentially frauds. Jesus pinpoints where they lack—they lacked a relationship with Him. He simply says, "I never knew you." That verse is intimidating and thought-provoking, because it lets me know that it might not be necessarily important that I know Jesus, but more importantly that he knows me. So who are these folks that Jesus is talking about? In a word, they are those who have stayed servants way too long. This then is the most important question: does Jesus know me?

But with that above verse, what does that mean on a day-to-day basis, that Jesus knows me? Today, often churches emphasize that we need to "know God," but how does it work for him to know us? First, think about this in terms of relationships. With relationships, one can stay on the periphery or you can enter into the experience of the friendship. You can know only the facts about someone and yet miss the essentials of the person. You can allow yourself to enter into the relationship or be held back. Think of it this way—I can know a whole lot about a person, but not really know the person at all.

I will give you an example of someone I know; I've known him for about three years. I know that he drives a Ford Explorer, has dark hair, likes to eat Mexican food at least once a week, has been married for twelve years, has a kid who is in first grade, roots for the Michigan State Spartans during March Madness, works in the accounting field. This is the first level of knowing someone. You get the facts. At a deeper level, I don't know much more about him even though I have known him for nearly three years. For example, in terms of "knowing" this person: I think he is a good father; I think he has a decent marriage; and I think he is a Christian. The problem is—this is how close we have become, or better yet, how close, he has become to me. I really don't know him at all. For the most part he has only given me so much about knowing him, and that has not been much at all. For all intents and purposes, even though I see him on a fairly consistent basis, we are acquaintances and not friends. On the flip side, I have opened up to him a little bit about myself. I have shared beyond the facts and shared with him some of my more personal stuff in an attempt to deepen our friendship. To put it simply, He knows me; but I don't know him. I think this is what Jesus is trying to get at with that passage. We can know a lot about him, but in the same breath, not really know him at all. We can engage regularly with him (i.e., go to church every Sunday or read our Bible daily), but never vulnerably open up our life to him. I think what Jesus was getting at in this passage is that those who are like this hold back a substantial part of themselves from God and from others.

So with this, a trademark of a person who is just a servant is often held back in terms of their relationship with God. How do I know this? First, I know this because I was like this at one point in my life. Even now, I can sometimes continue to be held back in terms of my relationship with God—holding it at the periphery. Because of this personal experience, I can also see that aspect in others when working with them as a pastor or counselor. Remember every single day you need to decide—will I be "just" a believer in Jesus, "just" a servant, or today will I continue to move into a friendship with him. It is important that we know Jesus; but it is life-changing and vital that he knows us.

Here are some tough questions you may have to ask yourself. Ask yourself: are you simply acquainted with Jesus or do you genuinely know him? Are you simply following some of the rudimentary rules of being a Christian or are you actually engaging the living God? As the example I used above, do you just know a lot of stuff about God, but in reality really don't know him? If this is the case, moving beyond just knowing Jesus, how can you let him know you? How can you better open up your life to him? We will get to one of these ways in an up-coming chapter.

DIAGNOSED WITH ATELOPHOBIA

We unwittingly project onto God our own attitudes and feelings toward ourselves... But we cannot assume that He feels about us the way we feel about ourselves—unless we love ourselves compassionately, intensely, and freely. Brennan Manning

A predominant characteristic of the behavior that I call evil is scapegoating. Because in their hearts they consider themselves above reproach, they must lash out at anyone who does reproach them. They sacrifice others to preserve their self-image of perfection. F. Scott Peck

Have no fear of perfection—you'll never reach it. Salvador Dali

Atelophobia, you might wonder, is the fear of not being perfect. This can often be the challenge of the person who has been a Christian, but never has really learned God's grace for themselves. Sadly, this can often be the chief problem of the person who has stayed a servant too long. The process of being a Christian can often have some dangerous marking points—after getting a few years under your belt, you are soon placed in a role of leadership—perhaps you're teaching Sunday school, perhaps you're leading a small group, perhaps you are pastoring a church of three thousand. As this begins to happen, people will begin to look up to you. They begin to have high expectations. They will applaud your service and your life. They will think you have it all together. But in reality, deep-inside, there might be significant problems attacking you from each side and because you feel compelled for some reason, you keep on playing the part of the "good Christian." Perhaps, you think, maybe you should be looked up to. Maybe, you should be applauded. Pretty much, you begin to feel like you do have to have it all together. Or that's what you tell yourself. However, there is another truth behind your mask:

- A seemingly benign struggle with depression has become

problematic in your life.
- A recent bout of chest pains which your doctor tells you is because of anxiety and stress has slowly built up in your life.
- You are fighting the present negative psychological ramifications of growing up in a family in which you were never told you were loved and worthwhile.
- You have developed an inability to feel any emotion which is creating havoc with your spouse.
- You have a sexual relationship with your spouse which is less than fulfilling and you begin doing things which at one point in your life you would have deplored.
- You verbally assault those around you on a regular basis and this anger seems to come out of nowhere.

As time goes on, you fail to deal with your brokenness inside, because you are not allowed to be broken, because you are a leader at church in some capacity or simply because you profess to call yourself a Christian. Christians don't have problems, right? You feel a hollowness inside, but as time goes on there is not the room in which to really look at your life and expose those places which need to be dealt with in your life. If you did, everyone would know the real you and that wouldn't be good. If this is where you find yourself, this is what Jesus calls building your house on sand. (Matthew 7:24-27)

There are often many moments in our lives in which God shines a light on our dark places and asks us to deal with these scary places in our lives. At this moment, it is up to us to dig at that area and unearth the deep-set sin or the deep wound from years past. No one is exempt—each of us are broken and God so much wants us to deal with that brokenness. With each of us, we have done great wrong in our lives in some capacity and God wants us to acknowledge that and begin to make amends with him, with others and with ourselves. With each of us, in some way, whether great or small, we each bring a woundedness to our lives. With this bruised part of our selves, each of us has learned to respond in negative ways in which we hurt others and bring harm to ourselves. We need to go back to the beginning and look at our lives and face those places which have brought harm to us so that we can heal.

- It's okay to go see a counselor about when you were sexually abused at age eight or because of a marriage that is deeply dissatisfying.
- It's okay to tell someone that you can trust that you are developing a drinking problem and your anger is destroying your life in subtle ways.

In terms of those I have counseled, a lot of folks I have seen simply do not deal with who they are and what their lives have become. They gloss over or deny the problems that they are facing in themselves, their marriages or families. For those who have glossed over their problems, often these folks are Christians. We are really good at doing that because we have this propensity to feel that we have to "Be perfect as your heavenly Father is perfect." (Matthew 5:48) We take a verse like that and misinterpret what it is trying to say. The verse offers us a good goal, but it is not supposed to be a standard we are to meet day-to-day. In this context, a better verse for us to remember is found in the book of James. Therefore, confess your sins to each other and pray for each other so that you may be healed. (James 5:16) We need to come clean about our lives with others and be honest with others about where we stand. Only then, this verse states, can we find healing.

Here is a suggestion with this issue. When I became a psychologist one of the challenges that our profession requests of each therapist is that we also open up our lives to seeking some help from a fellow counselor. It is first for our own mental and emotional health and also so we have first-hand experience in what it is like to go to counseling. I have done this and it was very rewarding and helped me sort through some problem spots I have had in my own life. I truly believe that everyone should try it at least for a short season in their lives. To have someone who is unbiased offering you good direction in your life can never be a bad thing. While it is important to find a gifted and skilled Christian counselor, I think that anyone can benefit from going and talking to someone about where they have wanted to make a change or where there has been a consistent problem in their lives. Counseling is founded on the importance of confidential conversations, and therefore, is a place where you might be able to share some things you've never shared with anyone. Maybe you should give it a try. Maybe it will be the first time where you were allowed to share the real you.

AN IMPORTANT INGREDIENT THAT'S MISSING

If you lose the joy and the fun, why bother? Jack Heffron

I remember someone once saying that joy is the hallmark of being a Christian. Another characteristic of what it means to be caught in the phase of the servant with regard to your faith is that this person has a lack of joy in their lives. This is one of the main missing ingredients when you get stuck in your faith—it's often joy that is missing. But what exactly is joy? First, from a biblical standpoint, there are fifteen different Hebrew words and eight Greek words to describe joy. From a grammatical standpoint, it is both a noun and a verb—I can have joy and I do joy.

As I have said, there are many words for joy in the Bible, but perhaps my favorite is the Hebrew ranan. For me, this word encapsulates the broad scope and the meaning of joy. It simply means to overcome or to cry out in exaltation or distress. The part I like is the aspect of being overcome by something. Here I can think of what was happening to me internally on my wedding day. I was overcome by the experience—something special was happening when I committed my life to Julie. It was a beautiful day. It was an intense day. It was unlike any other day that I have experienced. The picture of that moment in time for me is what it means to be a follower of Jesus in so many different ways. I mean think about it this way—what exactly happens to us when Jesus enters our lives full-blown? What might be an analogy of what happens to me when I give my life to him? When joy happens, this is what happens to me—I am overcome by his joy. Did you know that key character quality of God is joy?

Joy then is simply the possibilities of what it means to have a growing relationship with your Creator. Often we might think of joy as pleasure; but it's not that. A word that I think of when I think of the word joy is abandon. To understand this, let's go back to my wedding day and use an analogy of our sexuality. Sex is good and fun and pleasurable, because it's all about abandoned intimacy at its core. It's about entering this dramatically intense and intimate experience with your spouse. It's becoming yourself. It's about becoming the other person. Spiritually and physically, the Scriptures describe it as the two becoming one (Mark 10:8). Beyond the physical pleasure, to experience sex in its purest form is a soul-pleasure at its core. The best sex is when you get lost in your spouse, and yet at the same time, you become yourself in that intimacy. You touch a place in yourself like never before. Emotionally and spiritually, you go to another place like never before, and you understand another person like never before.

Joy is similar. But it is way beyond the feeling of pleasure. Joy is feeling good, but it's also consistent and deeply experienced. It is natural. It's inside you. You feel good about yourself. You know that God is confident in you, and that you are confident in him. Jesus is our model with this, and therefore, because he was a man of tremendous joy, we can do the things he did because of his overwhelming confidence in his Father, but also because of the Father's confidence in him. Jesus guides us when he says, "I tell you the truth, anyone who has faith in me will do what I have been doing. He will do even greater things than these." (John 14:12) You can walk on the water. You can tell the mountains to take a step to the left and move out of your way. You can move into someone's life and bring life-changing restoration. So let's summarize:

- First, joy is about rejoicing. It's celebration.
- Second, joy is about entering into an experience full-heartedly.
- Third, joy has an intensity about it. Joy = passion.
- And lastly and most importantly, joy allows people to be themselves, really themselves.

DON'T HAVE JOY?
THIS IS WHAT YOU GET IN RETURN

Do not use a hatchet to remove a fly from your friend's forehead.
Chinese proverb
Always do right. This will gratify some people and astonish the rest.
Mark Twain

Let's take another tactic and look at the opposite of joy. From what we've learned about joy, looking at the opposite, someone who might be joyless would be:
- Someone who sees the glass as half-empty.
- Someone who cannot be themselves.
- Someone who is stingy with their love, laughter and life.
- Someone who does not have emotional sensitivity.
- Someone who doesn't know how to have fun.
- Someone who has not experienced grace and freedom.
- And then finally, someone who tries to put all of that stuff above on other people.

For now were going to call the opposite of joy a term you may have heard of—for now, we'll call it legalism. Simply put: only living by the law is the opposite of joy. When we think of legalism, we might think of someone who puts a lot of rules on themselves and on others. But what is at the core of all of those rules? Why do people become legalistic? One definition explains that legalism is "strict adherence to the law, especially the stressing of the letter of the law rather than its spirit." Ray Stedman puts it in another way:

> Do you see how subtle [legalism] can be? The actual behavior can be exactly the same in the case of a legalist or of one behaving as an authentic Christian...It is what

is going on inside that is the issue in question. It is a matter of inner reliance...Legality on the other hand "is a mechanical and external behavior growing of our reliance on self, because of a desire to gain a reputation, display a skill, or satisfy an urge to personal power. . . . It is religious performance, scrupulous and meticulous in its outward form, but inwardly, as Jesus described it, 'filled with dead men's bones.

I love that final line: legalism is "religious performance, scrupulous and meticulous." When we talk about legalism, it's very hard to catch, because of that very word—*performance*. Let me explain. As one example, there are some actors who are almost too good at what they do. If you speak with some famous character actors who regularly play villains on television, they often say that people will come up to them on the street and say very unkind things to them. This is because these folks can't differentiate between the actor and the person; that's how good they are at acting! This is precisely the legalistic person; they are very good at acting like a Christian.

And here is where problems can arise—it is difficult not only for the innocent bystander, but also for the "legalistic" person to recognize their own legalism. Because a person's actions are the basis for what it means to be a Christian, everyone involved can be clueless. Sin is not easily quantified or seen, and it can be easy to miss in any person. When you look on the outside of most people, it may look like they are perfect and without any faults. Let's get one more quote in here to get a clear picture. I like what Mortimer Adler had to say about the issue:

> Sin is not only manifested in certain acts that are forbidden by divine command. Sin also appears in attitudes and dispositions and feelings. Lust and hate are sins as well as adultery and murder. And, in the traditional Christian view, despair and chronic boredom—

unaccompanied by any vicious act—are serious sins.

Again, it can be very easy to act like a Christian. Remember earlier when we said you could play a part or role? We are now going back to the checklist principle of determining who is a Christian and who is not. However, Jesus said that that is really hard to do, because you never really know what is going on inside of a person (Matt 23:25-28). Legalism is simply a checklist salvation, and since you have enough good deeds marked off, you are good to go and therefore, you must be right with God. If all the outward signs are visible then everything must be okay, right?

There are many examples of those who were legalistic in the Bible. Let me give you a scene from the Old Testament that exemplifies someone entering into joy and someone who is being held back. This exchange is a perfect example of the joyful and the joyless person, the one who has an authentic relationship with God and the other one who does not. This exchange is between David and Michal which we find in the Old Testament (II Samuel 6).

Let me set the story. David has been recently made king and he is now bringing back the Ark of the Covenant to Jerusalem. It's a really good day. It's time to celebrate. It's time to boogey-down. God is about to literally make his home in Jerusalem. The Scriptures detail an important scene from the day:

> Wearing a linen ephod, David was dancing before the Lord with all his might, while he and the entire house of Israel were bringing up the ark of the Lord with shouts and the sound of trumpets. As the ark of the Lord was entering the City of David, Michal, daughter of Saul, watched from a window. And when she saw King David leaping and dancing before the Lord, she despised him in her heart. (II Samuel 6:14-16)

In this scene, David is experiencing abandon. He's experiencing passion, freedom, joy unspeakable. God is now going to hang out with him and he knows things are going to be good, really good. He is deep in celebration and is overcome by what has occurred to him in the past years when God protected him and what is about to happen in his future. On the other hand, Michal is frozen and seeing this display of celebration and affection in her husband, it makes her sick to her stomach. The real God who wants to enter her life—this God she does not want. She wants only the God of her traditions, the one where she can stay at a distance. What she is doing has nothing to do with celebration. As the Scriptures detail "she criticized him for acting in a way unbecoming to a king." (2 Samuel 6:20) She even goes on to exclaim: "How the king of Israel has distinguished himself today, disrobing in the sight of the slave girls of his servants as any vulgar fellow would!"

Doesn't this sound like something we might hear today? Again, here's David abandoning himself to joy and worship; he's profoundly excited about what is happening and about what is going to happen. It is a sacred moment that Michal can't see or experience. God is going to turn everything around for Israel; everything is going to be profoundly different, and yet Michal is saying, *Come on David can't you have a bit more decorum! Please be respectable. Straighten up! Fix your tie! Please, be an adult.*

And rightly so, David doesn't want to—he wants to be child-like in his worship toward God—giving it his all and maybe not necessarily following all the rules and guidelines of 'proper' worship. He simply wants to celebrate. However, Michal can't see the value in David's worship to God. She only is able to value the thing that he represented—his position and his power—not as the man who shows complete devotion and abandon to his God. I love David's comeback.

> David said to Michal, 'It was before the LORD, who chose me rather than your father or anyone from his house when he appointed me ruler over the LORD'S people Israel—I will celebrate before the LORD. I will

become even more undignified than this, and I will be humiliated in my own eyes. But by these slave girls you spoke of, I will be held in honor.' (2 Samuel 6:21-22)

David says some important things here. First, he challenges, "I am not going to simply follow the traditions of your father in how I do things. I am going to be myself, loving God as I always have—in my own skin and in my own strange and peculiar way." Next, he challenges Michal by telling her, "Honey, I gotta be me and if that means becoming unbecoming or what you believe to be improper in my worship of God, so be it." Essentially, he's saying *Yes, I may be different in how I show my love to God. But Michal, I can't hold back like you have been used to doing.* By making this statement, he foreshadows Peter's own words centuries later—that he is a peculiar person and in this unique and extraordinary way, he will be entirely given to joy (I Peter 2:9).

THE SCRIPT FOR SELF-HATRED

When we are unable to find tranquility within ourselves, it is useless to seek it elsewhere.

Francois de La Rochefoucauld

A person is, among all else, a material thing, easily torn and not easily mended.

Ian McEwan

Those caught in this servant phase of faith have a basis of life which sadly often begins in self-hatred. Have you ever met someone like Michal; someone who is really legalistic and is resolved to follow all rules and decorum, no matter what the cost? The perfect character we might think of is the Church Lady that Dana Carvey played some years ago on Saturday Night Live. Do you remember her stammer, "Well, isn't *that* special…". Enid Strict is the uptight, smug, and pious host of her own talk show, 'Church Chat.' She's bogged down by do's and don'ts, and at the end of the day is only motivated by fear. She shows no joy, but only a dour, snooty, self-righteousness. In her bland and overly-patterned dresses, she is desperately lost from the One she seeks to follow. Sadly, the real Jesus is lost to her. Her only reliance is on a myriad of checklists; her only salvation is simply to NOT do a bunch of things that she deems sinful. And if you think about it, it's not so much what she does that makes her a Christian; rather what she won't do (and what you shouldn't either). The Church Lady is a perfect caricature of the person caught in the servant stage of faith.

Brennan Manning in his many books has a thing or two to say about joylessness and especially, this topic, self-hatred. Listen to how he pictures the joyless person—I like how he states it here because he captures for us what is at the core of these troubling issues.

> Even the compulsive drive for spiritual perfection, born
> not of the Spirit of God but as the needs of this world,
> only adds another scenario to the script for self-hatred.

In this quote he seems to say that striving for spiritual perfection at its foundation is about self-hatred. A person who is bound by rules and regulations are really suffering from a hatred of self. Again, on some level this person does not really know God's love because if they did, they wouldn't hate the person they are. But because of this self-hatred, they need to find ways in which to feel good about their lives. This is it. This is the starting point of what it means to be a servant too long—self-hatred. Go back to the Church Lady—isn't that what she is all about—self-hatred? She is no different than the Pharisees for whom Jesus had the harshest words.

But what is self-hatred and how can that manifest in a person? Think about it this way—anyone who is disconnected from God has some form of self-hatred. One cannot be disconnected from their Creator and at the same time, feel good about their life overall—at least not genuinely. Now, on the surface it may seem like a person may be happy or have it all together, but in reality they are masking with other things that help them to feel good about their lives. All kinds of people do this all the time; they use either wealth or people or what they do to give them this buffer. And guess what, you can also use religion to do this as well. When a person does not fully understand God's love for themselves, it is possible that they are still living a life alienated from God. While they may use the practices of religion and will tell you all about their 'relationship' with God, this can be a total sham. This person uses religion as a way in which to feel good about themselves and to create that feeling of being connected to something. Again, this can sometimes be very difficult to detect, because on the surface this type of person seems to be doing everything by the book. Some of these examples might be:

- They make it point to tell you that they waited until marriage before having sex. However, they fail to mention they did everything else before getting married…
- They know the Bible inside and out. They read it every day and have done so for the last ten years. The problem is that they never apply what they read to their lives…
- They faithfully serve in the children's ministry at your church and have perfect attendance. You don't know it, but behind closed doors, they yell at their children in a way that would make your blood curdle…

The marking point for a person who struggles with self-hatred and legalism is that they have yet to experience God's grace. This person may know the concept of grace and its definition, but they have yet to *experience* it for themselves. Again, this goes back to the idea that someone can know something in their head, but not in their heart. St. Silouan has a wonderful quote here that fits perfectly. He states, "He who does not love his enemies has not yet known God's grace." This is where everything hangs in the balance, because for the person who struggles with legalism, essentially, they themselves are the enemy and they have never learned how to love that person. This then becomes the starting and ending point. Until this person faces the reality that God genuinely loves them and they can't do anything to earn that, they will continue to work the cycle of "being a good person:" 1) self-hatred, 2) the habit of secret sins, 3) guilt and condemnation, 4) covering these sins with the appearance of "right" living, instead of being open about where they struggle. Sadly, on and on the cycle continues.

IS YOUR CHUCH SPIRITUALLY ABUSIVE?

Just as a person can be healthy or unhealthy, so can churches. Are you involved with a legalistic or spiritually-abusive church? Here might be some clues that you should mull over:

- At the heart of it, the overall message throughout the ministry that is spoken on a weekly basis is that God is a bookkeeper, keeping a checklist of do's and don'ts. He is impersonal and maybe even vindictive. If you mess with him, he's going to get you. The religion and experience is based on fear and not on grace. The church overly emphasizes and talks about sin (either about your sins or of others, but never of the church leadership). Overall, you often leave church feeling like you are always missing the mark, just aren't good enough, and you need to do more.
- The church strongly emphasizes doctrinal or theological correctness. They overemphasize minor theological issues which in reality seek to divide other churches or Christian groups from theirs. These theological issues may include baptism, the spiritual gifts, which Bible translation you should read, etc. This may even lead to the message that they are the only "true" church and other churches or Christians are misguided. This may be literally spoken from the pulpit or subtly suggested in other ways. Leaders or the church as a whole exhibit a spiritual arrogance—other churches are not quite as good as theirs and are missing the mark.
- Scripture is said to be of primary importance, but if you listen carefully, it is really the leader's *interpretation* of Scripture that is essential. The Bible isn't the end-all, rather the leader's ideas about what they think the Bible says is what is important. With this, the leadership tends to often teach that submission to authority is crucial to being a "good Christian."

- Religious traditions of the church are of utmost importance and biblical passages are used to mandate these traditions. Scripture is often misquoted or used out of context. Verses are singled out and used to substantiate the church's position on issues they hold dear. These verses are not weighed against what other verses say, which may suggest a different view. The context or the overall message of the Scriptures is not allowed.
- The church staff and leadership may be dominated by family members or personal friends. There is a lack of objective accountability: leadership is accountable to itself only and if any criticism about this is offered, it is shut down immediately. Intellectual development is limited to fit the doctrines that are taught at the church; schools or classes offered by other churches or organizations have little, if any worth and you should probably steer clear of "these types of people." There are two types of dysfunctional churches in these cases. Some churches may overemphasize the intellect (doctrine over experience); others may distrust anything "bookish" or intellectual and rely only on the experiences of the person (experience over doctrine).
- Church members or attendees who do not conform to all these doctrinal issues or opinions are blacklisted, labeled as rebellious or ignored for leadership positions. If you don't fully agree with the leadership, you have no voice and may even be asked to leave the church.
- Personal and emotional boundaries are often over-stepped and relationships can become too close. The leadership asks you to be vulnerable emotionally, but they themselves rarely, if ever, show or discuss any weaknesses. These leaders have the prototypical Savior-complex. If you ask them about their own struggles, they always seem to avoid the question.

These are just some of the possible traits of a spiritually abusive church. If you believe this may be the case for you, you may want to read one or two of the following books to learn more about this important topic:

- *Toxic Faith*, Stephen Arterburn
- *Tired of Trying to Measure Up*, Jeff VanVonderen
- *Healing Spiritual Abuse: How to Break Free from Bad Church Experiences*, Ken Blue
- *Bring 'Em Back Alive: A Healing Plan for those Wounded by the Church*, Dave Burchett

THE OXYMORON - SAINT AND SINNER

Lilies that fester smell far worse than weeds. Shakespeare

Man, when perfected, is the best of animals, but when separated from law and justice, he is the worst of all. Aristotle

Do you know the word oxymoron? It's a great little word. An oxymoron simply describes two aspects which seem opposite, but in ways, can be similar. It's something that seems like a contradiction on the surface, but in the end, both aspects can be true. We normally can find oxymorona in phrases. Let me show you some of my favorite examples:

- restless sleep
- random order
- new tradition
- modern history
- cold sweat

Here's another oxymoron. You are an oxymoron. You are a saint and sinner. That is an oxymoron. Let me explain:

1. When you become a Christian, you become this completely unique person. You are no better than anyone else, but in God's eyes, you are perfect, holy and righteous. You are a saint.
2. At the same time, you are no different than anyone on planet Earth. At times, you act like Mother Theresa and in others, you act in awful ways. You have a tremendous propensity toward sin and doing awful things. At a moment's notice, you could do some of the vilest things anyone has ever done—you are imperfect and unholy. You are a sinner.

When you get a chance, go listen to some of the music of Sufjan Stevens. He is a very gifted musician who writes songs that are not overtly "Christian," but his music is some of the most beautiful and

THE END OF ALL OUR EXPLORING

unique music I've listened to that are dedicated to themes of faith. On his album *Illinoise*, he has a song entitled John Wayne Gacy, Jr. You should find a copy and give it a listen.

If you don't know the story of John Wayne Gacy—he was this seemingly normal guy who lived in the suburbs of Chicago, but who also murdered countless young men, burying most of them in the crawlspace of his house. When he was arrested in 1978, his neighbors were shocked to learn who he really was —no one suspected him of these heinous crimes. After this happened, Gacy in the public's eye became the epitome of evil. I was a child at the time and can remember watching WGN news in Chicago each night and hearing of his horrific crimes. As a kid, there was no one scarier than John Wayne Gacy.

In the lyrics of his song about Gacy, Sufjan Stevens recounts all of these evil things he did and early on in the song, you get the sense that the song is just going to be how wicked Gacy was as a person. The song is haunting and I remember the first time I listened to it, sitting on the edge of my seat wondering where he would take the lyrics. In the last part of the song, Sufan Stevens through his words throws you for a loop and I remember being startled by the ending. This is how it ends:

And in my best behavior, I am really just like him;

Look beneath the floorboards, for the secrets I have hid.

I was shaken by his final words. The song seems to imply that each of us is capable of doing awful and evil things, and in reality, we each have a John Wayne Gacy in us. As the song ended, I was a bit astonished. *Me? I am like John Wayne Gacy?* After thinking about it, I now tend to agree. You see, I am capable of doing anything. You put me in the right circumstance, I would probably do anything: murder, adultery, you name it. I am capable of doing anything. And if I say I am not, I am either lying or in denial. As the famous hymn declares, "I'm a sinner without one plea."

This is the problem. The Bible states the same truth about who we can be. On the one hand, the Scriptures say that we are a new creation (2 Corinthians 5:17). You are totally different than before you gave your life to God. You are a saint. You are holy. You are righteous. But then on the other hand, you also have Paul in the New Testament, who for all intents and purposes in my eyes is the most dedicated Christian that we find in all of the Bible and he makes two remarkable comments about himself. At one point, he says he desires to do what is right, but often doesn't seem to follow through, is caught by sin, and often does the wrong thing (Romans 7:12-20). He essentially is saying that he knows how to sin really well and sometimes he just doesn't know how to stop. And yet, he doesn't stop there. Paul goes on to state in another passage that he is the very worst sinner that has ever lived. Essentially, he is saying he's worse even than John Wayne Gacy, Jr.

> Here is a trustworthy saying that deserves full acceptance: Christ Jesus came into the world to save sinners—of whom I am the worst. But for that very reason I was shown mercy so that in me, the worst of sinners, Christ Jesus might display his unlimited patience as an example for those who would believe on him and receive eternal life. (I Timothy 1:15-16)

When I read this, my initial thought is this—Paul is worst guy that ever lived? He's the best of the best of sinners?! I don't think so. That can't be right. But those are Paul's own words and not mine. Here, you have this hero of the Bible stating that he is even worse than John Wayne Gacy, a man who was a serial killer. On the one hand, you have a saint; on the other, a really really bad guy. This is Paul. That is a biblical example of an oxymoron: saint and sinner. Both one and the same.

However, often those who are caught in the servant phase of being a Christian have difficulty living in this tension of being both saint and sinner. As the great Brazilian novelist Clarice Lispector wrote in one of her stories "Who hasn't asked himself, am I a monster or is this what it means to be human?" Say this to yourself: *If you put me in the right circumstance and without the help from God at my side, I could do horrible and evil things.* This is a truth and unless you admit that, you will always live in this danger zone. You see, this is exactly what happened to Peter. Right before Jesus is to brought to be murdered, he tells his disciples what is about to happen and that each of them will disown him. Peter is the first and only to shout: *Jesus, I will never betray you—these guys might, but not me. It's just not in me. I will be good; you wait and see.* However, Jesus shakes his head in disagreement and simply says, Oh, how wrong you are, Peter. You shall see. We all know the end to that story, don't we? Again, when we read about Peter in the gospels, he is living just as a servant and not as Jesus' friend. As it applies to this, Brennan Manning wrote, "The temptation of the age is to look good without being good." In Peter's time, it was no different.

If one thinks about it this way, one of the most important "rules" that Jesus put on those who followed him was that if they were to deny him before other people, this relationship with him would be broken.

But whoever disowns me before others, I will disown
before my Father in heaven. (Matthew 10:33)

Jesus is basically saying if you do this one thing (i.e., deny being in a relationship with him to others), it is the Great Sin that is unpardonable;it is the one thing you can do to break the relationship between him and you. In this scene, Peter is insisting that he will keep that bargain. But we all know that didn't quite pan out for him and on some level, he betrayed Jesus no different than Judas. But that discussion is for another day and we will flush that issue out a little bit more in an up-coming chapter...

KEEPING A SAFE DISTANCE

Everyone has three lives: a public life, a private life, and a secret life.
Gabriel Garcia Marquez

In our society, most of us wear protective masks of various kinds and for various reasons. Very often the end result is that the masks grow to us, displacing our original characters with our assumed characters.
Clarence John Laughlin

As we take this topic one step further, remember how earlier we discussed the importance of Jesus "knowing" us (Matthew 7:23). As a parallel, a good question to ask yourself is how many people know the real you? In one aspect for Jesus to know us means that we must also let others into our lives in vulnerable ways. Jesus makes this remark, "I have spoken to you of earthly things and you do not believe; how then will you believe if I speak of heavenly things?" (John 3:12) I think in the same way, one of the best ways that Jesus can know us is how well we let others know who we are. In tandem, just as we attempt to develop a relationship with God (i.e., a heavenly relationship), we must also push into friendships with those around us (i.e., an earthly relationship). Typically, on this front, those caught in the servant stage have a long way to go.

This is another way to find out if you might be caught in this servant phase with regards to your relationship with Jesus. If so, there's a good chance that you limit your friendships to acquaintances in your life. The question you have to ask yourself is—how deep do I go in my relationships? How much do people know the real you? How many people know for example that you struggle with lust at an extreme level, or you periodically slap your kids, or your marriage is maybe just one or two fights away from a separation? Those who keep others at bay, usually keep God at bay in some manner as well.

And often these types of shallow relationships flourish in a church setting. As a metaphor, too often, going to church means we are going to the symphony, when in reality, going to church should be more like when you go to a hospital in an emergency. If we were to go to the symphony, we would put on our best jacket or dress, blow dry our hair just perfectly, and put our best smile on to impress. But church is not like going to an orchestra concert; it should be more like going to a hospital.

Some years ago, one December day, I was getting the mail and walking down our driveway. I slipped on an icy patch and down I went. As I fell, I used my left arm to brace my fall and just then, I felt my elbow twist like it never had before. I laid on the ground for a second and was wondering what had just happened. That left arm was in excruciating pain. I lifted myself up and realized I had done something very bad to my arm as I could not straighten it. It hurt like nothing I had ever experienced. Julie was on her way home and I called her in painful cries. Once she got home, she immediately drove me to the hospital. However, before all this had happened, I had yet to take a shower and I had yet to change from what I had slept in the night before. This is how I entered the emergency room that day. I was in pain. I needed help. My hair was unwashed. I did not have on my Sunday best. The real Kelly Bonewell had entered that emergency room, because I needed help, and I needed it now. This was the real me for all to see. In a way, this is what going to church should be like. Not like going to the symphony, but more like entering the emergency room to receive help where you are allowed to be the real you.

Too often, when we are at church we play a part, but we don't let anyone know the real story behind our lives. People ask us how we are doing, but we quickly reply, Oh, fine. But are we really doing fine? In fact, the truth maybe is that we've made a mess of our lives and only we know it. We maybe are moments from doing something really stupid and nobody in our lives knows the truth of that.

Early in my journey in being a Christian, I had a startling experience with this aspect of going only so deep. After becoming a Christian, I was desperate to find a church, because I wanted to know others who also knew this Jesus person. I had been told you can find people like these in churches… One day, I was going to class on the train into Chicago and as I flipped open my green Gideon's New Testament this red-headed guy sat next to me. He quickly asked me if I was a Christian because he noted the book I was reading. I told him I was and over the course of that twenty minute ride on the train, we talked. Right before he was about to get off at his stop, he invited me to his church. I was grateful and excited.

Over the next year, I became highly involved in this tiny little church which met in this huge old church building in Oak Park. I came into my own as a Christian and got to know the pastor of the church and his young family. During this time, I had heard a message that Tony Campolo spoke which really impacted who I was to become as a Christian. He maintained in this message the vital importance of accountability with others in your walk of being a Christian. I remember one line in particular; as a paraphrase, he said, "Unless you become ultimately close with others and open up your life to them, you maybe will be sitting in a church pew in your old age, but you won't be a Christian." I really took that to heart and asked my pastor and some others to join me in living this life of being accountable with one another.

I can remember our first meeting and this is when my eyes were opened. We were a few guys at my pastor's office, sitting on furniture which had been bought at the local Salvation Army and with full coffee cups in hand. Because I initiated this little group, I began first and shared what was going on—I didn't hold back and shared the genuine struggles that were going on in my life. After that, two other guys did just as I had and shared with vulnerability the sin and struggles in their lives. When it came to my pastor, he looked us each one-by-one and said he appreciated what we shared, but at that point, he said, he really didn't have anything to share. Taken aback, our time together ended.

I walked away puzzled. He had nothing to share? As I spent the next couple years at that church, I slowly began to realize that this was my pastor's natural way of operating—he never really shared what was going on in his life whether that was from the pulpit or when we shared breakfast at our favorite diner. At the end of four years, I didn't know him much better than the guy who lived next door, who worked third shift and who I would wave and say hello to when we would pass in the hallway. After spending those four years at the church, I moved and therefore, had to find another church.

About six years later, we had a sort of reunion with a some who attended this church. During our time together, I learned that my pastor had left his wife and four kids. He literally packed up and moved to where no one knew where he had gone. He simply vanished. I was shocked. He literally left his wife and family? My pastor? And then it dawned on me, it kind of made sense. A lot of other stuff must have been going on in his life which he was just not dealing with and he just never let anyone into all of the secrets in his life.

Let me make an important statement—you will never grow as a Christian without the help of others. Those who think that they can live as followers of Jesus, but not have any relationships that mean anything are dead wrong. The way that God designed how we grow as a person is that we grow first because we have a developing relationship with him, but a close second, is because we enter into deep relationships with others. This is a good question to ask yourself—how well do others know the real you? How many genuine friendships do you have and how deep do they go? And here is an important point, you might have three thousand friends on facebook, but how well are you known? Can you count on at least one hand how many of your friends know most of the nooks and crannies of your life? The inevitable truth is this, if you have very few friendships that are authentic in your life, most likely your life has a shallowness to it. If you have very few deep friendships in your life, most likely you are not moving in the right direction. For some, if there are very few people in your life who can support you, you probably are a catastrophe waiting to happen.

DOING IT FOR THE CAUSE

We have been far too tolerant of pain and suffering when it isn't our own. We are far better at fixing parts than people, far better at saving souls than comforting sinners, far better at killing than carrying for the wounded. Thomas Lynch

We all need a mission or calling in life. God has given each of us a purpose which is grand and should be a focal part of our life. However, for some, the lifework of being a Christian can go awry and turn into something that it should not. Sometimes "being a Christian and serving the Lord" can actually become an idol. Sometimes the causes we become involved in can actually lead us into doing things that don't model anything that Jesus taught or exemplified.

I'll give you an extreme example of a "Christian group" who is doing it for the cause, but are missing the point entirely. Have you heard of the Westboro Baptist Church? This group epitomizes what it means to be a servant of Jesus way too long. They are a church (if you could call them that) known for its extreme stance against homosexuality and its protest activities, which include picketing funerals of those they believe are in the wrong in some way. You may have seen them on television or the internet; they are the group that has the signs that say *God Hates Fags*. Jon Stewart had an interesting comment about them, "The Westboro Baptist Church is no more a church than Church's Fried Chicken is a church." This group has a cause. This group is very passionate about its cause. However, its cause is also extremely misguided and hateful. In many ways, this group epitomizes the Pharisees of our day. I like what F. Scott Peck, the Christian psychologist said about such folks, while it may seem harsh, there is truth in his words about the danger of living for a cause and then letting it go awry:

Since they must deny their own badness, they must

perceive others as bad. They project their own evil onto the world. The evil attack others instead of facing their own failures. Strangely enough, evil people are often destructive because they are attempting to destroy evil. The problem is that they misplace the locus of the evil. Instead of destroying others they should be destroying the sickness within themselves.

In some ways, it's easy to be zealous. Whether its animal rights, a political agenda, or a religion, being obsessive in this sense simply means you need to be really passionate about your ideology. Anybody can do that and people become fanatical about different issues for countless reasons.

- People become zealous for a cause because of hatred.
- People become zealous for a cause because of a selfish motivation.
- People become zealous for a cause because of boredom.
- People become zealous for a cause because they feel they need a calling in their life.
- People become zealous for a cause because of ignorance.
- People become zealous for a cause because of loneliness.

As an example of this, I remember some years ago, a good friend had reached out to a guy who was in prison and he would help him lead a Bible study for some other inmates. This person who had been in prison for about three years had become a Christian since his incarceration and he had become very passionate about his faith. He loved sharing it with others; he loved studying the Bible; he wanted to always do the right thing. He was the ideal Christian or so everyone thought.

However, a couple of years later he got out of prison. Once he was released, he lost his zeal and passion for his faith, and instead placed that into things like motorcycles and women. He simply did this—he changed his passion from Jesus to these things. From the above list of reasons why people become passionate about a cause, some of the likely reasons he was so passionate about being a Christian was because he had selfish motivations, the loneliness of prison life, or simply because of boredom. Sadly, once he got out of prison, he simply transferred or changed his passions.

An example of this that we know from Scripture is through the story of Mary and Martha. This is how the story reads:

> As Jesus and his disciples were on their way, he came to a village where a woman named Martha opened her home to him. She had a sister called Mary, who sat at the Lord's feet listening to what he said. But Martha was distracted by all the preparations that had to be made. She came to him and asked, "Lord, don't you care that my sister has left me to do the work by myself? Tell her to help me!"
>
> "Martha, Martha," the Lord answered, "you are worried and upset about many things, but few things are needed—or indeed only one. Mary has chosen what is better, and it will not be taken away from her." (Luke 10: 38-42)

I love that line Jesus shares with Martha—"you are worried and upset about many things." Isn't that precisely what the Westboro Baptist Church is all about. They are worried that the great United States of America is going to hell in a hand basket. And they know who the culprits are, don't they—it's gay people! And this is who they picket with their *God Hates Fags* placards. Because of this, those caught in the servant stage of faith simply have not learned how to do a very important thing. Jesus alludes to it in the passage above. They don't know how to rest. Rest from their compulsion that they must always be doing something.

Again, obviously serving is a key component of being a follower of Jesus. Giving back to someone else in whatever capacity is vital in being a person of faith. But it is not who we are; it is just something we do in our gratefulness to God for what he has done for us. I always tell my sons that because our family has been blessed in many ways, we need to share these good things with others. It is the Christian way. But again, it is not who we are. We should never base our identity off our creeds, convictions or causes. First and foremost, we are God's child, and not his employee or hired hand. We should never feel that we are obligated to do something for God. Those who do that get caught in serving the cause and not their Maker.

To drive home this point, you have to go rent a movie. Have you ever seen the movie *The Great Santini*? It is a tremendous film on so many different levels. Robert Duvall plays a hard-nosed military pilot; in some ways he's Peter incarnate. Duvall is a man who is driven and everything has to be just right. He deeply desires that his wife and kids have the good life. However, he is also a man with a darkness about him. At different times in the film you see him verbally and physically assaulting his wife and his kids in epic proportions. He, in many ways, has all the right motives, but gets it entirely wrong as a father and husband. The film gives us a great perspective of what someone looks like when they have been a servant way too long. It is a great movie which depicts a man who loves his family, but in reality doesn't really love his family at all, because he is too passionate about being the perfect dad. In Duvall's character, he captures who Peter was at one time in his life, before Jesus dramatically teaches him about grace.

IT'S NOT MY FAULT!

Spiritual growth requires the acknowledgment of one's own need to grow. If we cannot make that acknowledgment, we have no option except to attempt to eradicate the evidence of our imperfection.

M. Scott Peck

When you work with people through counseling, you get this unique gift and responsibility in that you get to know people at a deep level. It's what I love about my job. That's exactly what I did 24-7 and in a way, I have been able to learn a lot about a lot of different people. Through these experiences, I have learned one thing very clearly, we are sinners; we all are tremendously fallen creations. You see, through counseling I have had the privilege to see all of a person's quirks, their misgivings, their disordered personalities. I get to hear it all and on the one hand, that is a benefit of being a counselor, but on the other, if you aren't careful in my work, it can make you a bit jaded. It's like being a police officer, doctor or nurse; you get to see the harsh and hard side of life. You know that part of you that slows to see a car collision; I would essentially slow down every day and get to see these emotional, spiritual and relational accidents every day. I have especially seen this dynamic of being open and vulnerable when I meet with couples whose marriages are falling apart. The wife or husband feels slighted and so they come in and lay it all on the line. In some cases, they totally let out all the darkness about the other person and you just kind of sit there and go, *Wow, now that's more information then I needed.* Often, when a person gets into counseling its no holds barred and they will share anything and everything with you.

So with that, let's ask that important question again—are you broken? And if so, how do you observe this? How do you deal with that truth? I usually find this at work—people either view themselves as completely without any fault or the worst person in the world without much of any hope. With a lot of us, there is no middle ground. I am either a saint. Or I am a sinner. For myself, genuinely in my heart, I sometimes don't see my sin so well and my brokenness is not always evident in my own eyes. In some ways, it is easier for me to see my goodness than my sin. In my business, we call that a blind-spot. However, with other people I meet, they only see themselves as destructive, mean and a wreck. Sometimes, it can be difficult to stay in that middle ground that I am both a saint and a sinner.

Again, going back to when I have done marriage counseling, this is the great danger. One partner is trying to change the other, because they genuinely believe the entire problem in the marriage lies in their partner's court. The problems and the failing marriage has little to do with them personally. Whenever I have counseled a couple like this, essentially each person is saying, *Kelly, if you can get this jerk to change, our marriage will finally be moving in the right direction.*

Yet sometimes when I am in this situation, if I were to challenge this person and ask them where they need to personally change, they most likely will just look back at me with a blank face. *Me?! You have to be kidding. I'm not the problem! She is!* People have a hard time realizing they are broken; that they are the problem. And when they do fail in real-time—meaning they were caught lying or threw the plate across the room or cheated the waitress out of her tip—they either beat themselves up beyond belief or simply rationalize the facts at hand that they have not done something wrong. How do I know about this dynamic? Because, I do it all the time. Why? Because just like you, I am broken as well and actually have gained a great degree of expertise at failing in my life. Again, as I said earlier, just like Paul, you and I are the worst of sinners (1 Timothy 1:15-16).

WHEN SOMEONE POINTS OUT YOUR WORST

Some years ago I went through this denial stuff and it was pointed out to me in a rather honest manner. Every Wednesday night, I would play badminton with a bunch of people. I love the game, because it's fast and yet at the same time almost anyone can pick up the game quickly. When I play anything, whether its badminton or a board game, I can become competitive. Sometimes, I almost don't know I'm being aggressive. Sometimes, I don't take other people's feelings into account, especially if I am playing a team sport. I can get grumpy; I can be challenging; I can be too authoritarian. One night, I was playing with a friend of a friend. We were getting beat pretty badly, primarily because we were not playing very well as a team. Playing doubles in tennis or badminton can be a challenge if you don't know exactly what the other person is doing. During the game, I was trying to tell this person who was new to the game where he needed to be on the court and where he needed to position himself. If we missed the point, I immediately turned to him and mentioned what went wrong. But midway through the game, we lost another point and I mentioned that he needed to go to the net on the play. He barked at me that he knew how to play and I didn't need to give him advice. At first I thought he was joking, but then he went on and basically said that I was being a jerk. He was harsh, man! I tried to apologize in a roundabout way, which really wasn't an apology at all and for the rest of the night we basically stayed to our own corners. As I drove home that night, I was wrestling with the incident. I was playing around with it in my mind, going over what I had done and what he had said. Basically, I just felt he was the jerk and taking the situation way too seriously. The whole incident in my mind was that it was his fault—that jerk!

About a mile from home, a still small voice spoke to me and it simply said this, *Kelly, you were the jerk… and often when you play badminton you are way too hard on people and way too competitive. Finally, someone called you out. You were the one at fault. And you didn't like that, did you?* The words were the voice of God or what some call our conscience. You know what, I didn't want to hear that. It was his fault—he was the one who spoke with vehemence. But guess what, God was calling out for me to look at my own sin. He wanted me to take ownership of myself. But I wanted to deny it, and when that didn't work, I tried to rationalize why I was the way I was. On the way home I came up with some pretty sound reasons:

- You should always do things with excellence.
- Even though winning isn't the most important thing, you should always try to play your best and as a team.
- I was the one who has been playing badminton longer; this guy should have been open to learning from me and learn to take a little criticism.

But God had something else in store; he wanted to confront me about my sin. I had to own my stuff and let that guy own what he had to own. And this is why he had to deal with this brokenness in me; this sin of control and pride didn't just come up on Wednesday night's playing badminton. These behaviors were a fairly common occurrence for me and happen all the time: with Julie, with my sons, at work, etc. On that drive home, God was seeing if I would admit what was obvious—that I needed to change in these areas of my life. It took awhile, but by time I reached for the garage door opener when I drove into our drive, I finally came clean and slowly began to look in the mirror.

It is very painful admitting that we are messed up, because someone else usually points these kinds of things out to us (e.g., your spouse, your kids, a co-worker, etc.). You should never be surprised that you make poor judgments and fail. I sometimes see this when I am counseling parents of young toddlers or children. Sometimes they are surprised that their kid is doing awful things like hitting another kid at school or talking back to them. Once the child gets older and is moving into adolescence, the parents begin to blame themselves. What did we do wrong? What could we have done differently? Why is she acting like this? I never raised him to be like this? All of this spells out how much free will we have as individuals. For example, no, your parents probably never sat down with you and taught you how to lie. *Okay now, son, if you want to learn how to lie, here are some pointers. First, always tell a lie with a straight face. It works better that way. Second, make sure you remember your lie or otherwise you might actually tell the truth and mess the whole thing up. And finally, son, if you are going to become a really good liar, you have to learn how to not feel bad that you are deceiving and manipulating people.*

This whole concept is very difficult for those stuck in the servant stage of faith to understand. On principle and on paper, they will acknowledge that they are broken. That is a given, but in the end, this becomes simply theological correctness: Jesus died for me, a sinner. Again, this sort of person knows it in their head, but not their heart. And this boils down to one truth. There is one very dramatic way you can tell if perhaps you or someone else has been a "servant" too long as it relates to all of this:

- You never say you are sorry.
- You rarely say that you are wrong.
- You are rarely, if ever, the one at fault.

This is especially true in our most intimate of relationships, with our wives or husbands, with our children, with those closest to us. Ask yourself that one question, how often do you find yourself saying you are sorry and really meaning it? If you as a person are uncomfortable with those words, there's a pretty good chance you are stuck in your faith as well. Those who have genuine friendship with Jesus are okay at being wrong, they are okay with stepping up and saying they are sorry. The person stuck in the servant stage of faith is not. They never say they are sorry; they are rarely in the wrong and if they are it is because of minor infractions. If a person is never apologizing in their life, they are living as if the cross meant nothing to them. One way to think about this is that it's easy saying you are sorry to God; how easy is it for you speak those words to those who are closest to you? Do you ever? Is it a once a year occurrence and even then the conversation ends by you blaming the other person for the wrong? *I'm sorry for calling you that name, BUT you shouldn't have made me mad!* That is no apology—that is you just blaming someone for your own sin patterns. Here is an exercise, when was the last time you said you were sorry to your husband or wife? Your son or daughter? Your good friend? If you can't remember, something might not be quite right.

WHEN THE BIBLE BECOMES AN IDOL

He says one thing, but he does another; it seems to me to be common sense to look at what is done, and not to what is said.
Billy Martin

The sacred page is not meant to be the end, but only the means toward the end, which is knowing God himself.
A. W. Tozer

Going back to looking at the life of Peter that we read in the gospels, it can teach us a lot. This is where he was living—he was living life bound by conventions—what is good and proper. Those caught in the stage of being just a servant have a mechanism which allows them to forget that they are broken people. To make themselves feel good about themselves, they put in place what psychologists call *coping mechanisms.* Coping mechanisms can be described as the different ways in which a person attempts to handle stress and difficulty in their lives. Sometimes these mechanisms we use can be unconsciously motivated, learned behaviors, or most often, skills we master in order to reduce stress or other intense emotions like guilt or depression. It's important to note that sometimes coping mechanisms are actually healthy ways in dealing with our problems and at other times, very detrimental. A common example of a coping mechanism would be someone who uses alcohol or sex to alleviate pain in their life. Obviously, both of these are negative coping mechanisms. Interestingly, one can use different aspects of their religion to deal with internal pain no different than a bottle of vodka or a one-night stand. The Bible, in this case, can actually become one of those coping mechanisms. Again, even though in theory, the person caught in this servant stage of faith knows that they cannot earn God's approval, deep down, they psychologically behave as if they can. This may come in the fashion of many different types of coping mechanisms which are disciplines of their faith. Some others might be: praying regularly, going to church, serving in some capacity, etc. Again, each of these disciplines are good in themselves, but the person stuck in the servant stage of faith uses them to temporarily alleviate pain of some kind, to feel good about themselves, and to try to create the allusion that God is pleased with them because they do these things. These types of aspects are chief to their relationship with God and it keeps the whole house of cards from falling. A little bit later we will discuss another dynamic in what this cycle looks like in a bit more detail.

Now don't get me wrong, I'm all for spiritual disciplines and guidelines on one level. And of course, the Bible is full of direction and practical guidance for our lives. Francis Schaeffer says this: "Doctrinal rightness is important, but only as a starting point to go on into a living relationship—and not as an end in itself." You see these rules that "servants" put together to accomplish the task of feeling good about themselves and excluding others are really simplistic, and on some level not a Christian way of doing things at all. So with this, the Bible becomes the arbiter for these rules and the manual that needs to be followed and strictly obeyed. For some Christians, the Bible then becomes an idol. What do I mean by that?

Before I begin by discussing that question, I need to declare that I firmly believe that the Bible is one of the cornerstones of our faith. Without it, we would not have the direction that we so desperately need in our lives and this is beautifully brought out in the story of Josiah that we find in its pages (2 Kings 22:1-23:30 and 2 Chronicles 34:1-35:27). Amazingly, Josiah became king when he was only eight years old. In contrast to other kings before him, the Bible is clear in declaring right from the start that "He did what was right in the eyes of the Lord." Some years later, when Josiah was in his mid-twenties an amazing thing occurred to him and to the nation of Judah. Up to this point, earlier kings had betrayed their faith in God and did many wicked things in how they lived their lives. Josiah was different and he tried to restore his relationship with God. The remarkable part of his story is that up to this point, the Scriptures had been literally lost. Can you imagine that— to not in any way shape or form to have the Bible to rely on and guide you? What would our lives look like today if this happened to us? Up to this point, Josiah was attempting to follow God, but he was doing it in the dark.

So back to the story. Not until Josiah requested that the temple be repaired does one of the priests miraculously find the lost Book. Even though up to this point, Josiah and the nation had been doing their best in following the commands of God, not until they re-discovered the Book of the Law did they fully realize how misled they were living. In the Old Testament, we read this (2 Kings 22:11-13):

> When the king heard what was written in the book, God's Revelation, he ripped his robes in dismay...He ordered them all: "Go and pray to God for me and for this people —for all Judah! Find out what we must do in response to what is written in this book that has just been found! God's anger must be burning furiously against us—our ancestors haven't obeyed a thing written in this book, followed none of the instructions directed to us."

Astonishingly, Josiah in his reading of these sacred words realizes they have not been keeping to the stories and commands of the Scripture. This story beautifully illustrates the vital nature of having the Bible in our lives and being able to hear its direction for how we are to live. Without a doubt, the Bible is indispensable and desperately needed in our lives. If we ever lose it in our lives, we will be lost.

WHEN THE BIBLE BECOMES A WEAPON

However, for some, the Bible becomes an instrument in which a person can first "use" it against themselves, and then eventually "use" it against others. The end goal then of reading the Bible is that the person who knows the most is the holiest. The Bible then becomes a weapon. Have you ever heard the phrase "knowledge is power?" In this case, this is a power that is corrupted. When one misreads the truth of the Bible, they inevitably corrupt themselves and others. What do I mean by all this? How does a person "use" the Bible against themselves and others in an unhealthy way?

The Bible is not a John Grisham novel. By no means is it an easy read. It is definitely not a book you can just flip through like you would a magazine. It takes great thought and prayer to be able to understand its truth (2 Timothy 2:15). The Bible is a book you must dedicate your whole life to, each and every day. The Bible is so rich and vital that you must create space in your life daily to understand what it is trying to say to you. You cannot always just open up the Scriptures and pick a verse and apply it to your life. How you view God; what you know about the historical context of the passage; how you apply that passage to other passages in the Bible—all of this impacts how you can interpret a passage in the Scriptures. Let me give you an example in terms of how a person might read the Bible and apply their own misconceptions of who God is. Listen to this verse:

> Therefore I will make the heavens tremble; and the earth will shake from its place at the wrath of the LORD Almighty, in the day of his burning anger. (Isaiah 13:13)

When reading a passage like this, if a person already associates God as their dad growing up—the guy who was always yelling and screaming; who physically abused them; who was never around—how do you think they will associate God when reading a passage like this? And if they do it with this passage, they will do it with countless others. And if they do it with countless other passages, the God who they envision is not the God who is merciful, forgiving, loving. The very Person who they imagine God to be, the central character of the Bible then becomes this crooked Person who with each page they turn, they begin to question why they believe in him in the first place. Once a person does this, the whole of the Bible then is impossible to read because the person does not understand the central truths of who God is: merciful, forgiving, loving. Is God other things like just and sometimes gets very angry and is jealous for us? Absolutely. But he is not the God who is always angry. Deep down, for some this is how they view God. He is never happy and always moping around, and at any moment about to blow a gasket. Those who are caught here, only see the God you can never please. And this is a very dangerous place to be. This is why that the person who does not genuinely know grace should probably be very careful in reading the Bible. Too often, they will misread it because of their predispositions and their past.

THE STERN FATHER

I do not want to be the inheritor of so many misfortunes. I do not want to continue as a root and as a tomb. Pablo Neruda

As I said earlier in the book, how we view God is all-important. It is the underpinning of our entire life. Most often, our view of God comes from two places in our lives: 1) from how we were raised, i.e., from our parents and our upbringings; and 2) what we are taught from others either directly or indirectly. Again, as we look at Peter's life, on a few different occasions, Jesus had to correct him in terms of his view of God (Matthew 16:23, John 13:3-9, Acts 10). Jesus completely understood that if Peter did not change some of these views, everything else would also get bent and distorted in his life. Jesus clearly saw this in the religious leaders of his time and he didn't want these same attitudes and behaviors to continue in Peter.

There is one common denominator when it comes to those who are stuck in this phase of faith of being the servant—they inevitably see God as the stern father—Someone who has expectations that can never be met. Now, none of this is out in the open; these views are emotionally held in the sub-conscious and in the deep part of the person's soul. This truly is how they see God—he cares very little for them. If you were to ask them to name some of God's characteristics they would be able to perfectly and even eloquently share with you these:

- God is good.
- God is gracious.
- God is loving.
- God is forgiving.

But in truth, to internally experience these realities on a daily basis, they don't even come close. Deep inside, deep within their soul, God is not good or loving or forgiving. And with this, here is a simple test in how you can determine how a person genuinely sees God—don't ask them how they view God—ask them how they view themselves. Don't let them think about the question just ask them for the first words that come to their mind. Inevitably, the person caught in this stage of faith will use the majority of their description with words such as these: a sinner, broken, wicked, evil, a fallen person. In how they view themselves, we begin to see a picture of how they might view God. They will not use true words such as these—righteous, saved, holy, redeemed, a child—such words would not be the ones that would first come to their mind.

Those who are caught in this servant stage of faith need to assess truly how they view God. They need to get beyond the simple mental conceptions that they have learned and look at who God is genuinely to them right now. But here is the tough part with this self-reflection—you often need someone else in your life who knows you extremely well to help you answer these questions of who God is to you. With the person who is stuck in this phase, as mentioned in a previous chapter, too often this is a no-no; you do not get close to others and you definitely don't need the help of others.

Often these deep-seated ideas of who God is began a long time ago in a land far, far away. Sometimes a person stuck here will need to deal with issues from the past and often these issues might be difficult to acknowledge or deal with because of the pain or confusion associated with them. Some of these difficult issues to address might be:

- How you were raised – especially growing up in home in which perfection was always required or where a parent was emotionally distant
- Being physically, emotionally or sexually abused in the past
- Facing a traumatic event that occurred in your life
- Having a parent who was extremely domineering or passive
- Growing up in a home that was overly religious (overly

emphasizing the rules of the faith over grace and forgiveness)

FACING THE WOUND OF REJECTION

There is an important concept from psychology that might help you understand one dynamic of this in terms of one's up-bringing. Gregory Bateson, a linguist and anthropologist, wrote in the 1950's about the concept of a *double bind*; it is a term that is used when children grow up with inconsistent and negative parental messages. Double binds usually are most damaging within the relationship of a parent to a child; however, they can also occur in different types of relationships such as with siblings, extended family relationships, within dating or marriage relationships and friendships. Here is the basic process of how a double bind occurs within the relationship of a parent and child:

- *Stage One: Confusion.* First, the child who experiences a double bind receives contradictory verbal and emotional messages when they are spoken to by their parent. For example, love is expressed by words, and yet disgust or detachment is exhibited by behaviors by the parent. Likewise, a child is encouraged to speak freely, but then criticized or silenced whenever they actually do share their view on a given issue.
- *Stage Two: Control.* Often, when such conversations occur, the child is not allowed to disengage from the conversation which has these conflicting messages.
- *Stage Three; Punishment.* Finally, if within the conversation, the child fails to fulfill the contradictory requests of the parent, they are punished in some way (e.g., withdrawal of love, physical punishment, verbal attacks, etc.).

The classic example given of a negative double bind is of a mother telling her child that she loves him, while at the same time turning away in disgust for some reason. In this case, the words the mother speaks are normal and good, but then the body language is in conflict with the words the mother just spoke. The child doesn't know how to respond to the conflict between the words and the body language and the harmful behaviors of the parent (this can be either physical or psychological). Overtime, the child in this case will become either very suspicious of those who attempt to show him love or will become very dependent on the parent or others.

Often those who grow up in religious homes experience double binds on a regular basis. It is the image of the parent who says "I love you," but in reality never really shows it in a physical manner or often shows their repulsion more times than not. It's the father who says to his daughter with his mouth "You are important to me," but never expresses it in a physical and tangible way.

I will share an example I heard recently. A client of mine shared an experience of a double bind which was very damaging and confusing to him. This man had been in an accident in which someone on a motorcycle had died because of their own reckless driving. It was not this young man's fault in any way, and he stayed at the scene of the accident. Obviously, it was a a very troubling experience for him. In his family, he was never allowed to express emotion and on different occasions was actually told to "stop crying" or to keep his feelings in check. One afternoon, he and his mom were in the same room and she pointedly asked, "I am really surprised how you haven't expressed any emotion about the accident last week. Hasn't it bothered you?" At that moment, a wave of emotion rushed over him and he began to cry. He reached for his mom to hug her and she pushed him away. This is a perfect picture of a double bind. Step by step, this is what happened:

1. Throughout his life, verbally and non-verbally, he was told not to show emotion.
2. In this incident, he initially did as he was told and did not show any emotion about the accident.
3. His mom requested that he show emotion about the accident.
4. He was rejected and punished for showing emotion.

If you grew up in a home like that, how do you think you would view God? You'd be very confused and it would make sense that how you grew up would influence who God was to you. This often can be the case with the person who is stuck in this legalistic stage of faith. Even without really knowing it, they have grown up in a highly dysfunctional home, experienced subtle abuse and then transferred this experience to their relationship with God. In the situation, with the young man above, this is how I found him when he came into counseling. He was highly distrustful of others and he was highly distrustful of God. Now granted, he went to church each Sunday and served in a lot of meaningful ways there, but in reality, he was a very broken young man who really needed to get at some root issues that had happened a long time ago. Not until he began to see the harm in his past was he able to begin to look at himself and others differently. This healing initially began in that he confronted the truth that he was beginning to mimic his mother's emotional distance with his own family. Second, he had to reach out for help—these two things were the beginning of his healing from a very wounding childhood and upbringing. Those caught in this servant stage of faith have a hard time doing what this young man did. Only those who are willing to look deeply at their past and how they are responding presently because of the past are able to grow in their relationship with God. The God who heals desperately wants us to deal with our wounds and often that means we must first acknowledge them.

WHEN FLIPPING ON THE RADIO CAN CHANGE YOUR LIFE

After loss of identity, the most potent modern terror, is loss of sexuality.
Jeanette Winterson

'The law of Jehovah is perfect, restoring the soul.' (Psalm 19:7). Most laws condemn the soul and pronounce sentence. The result of the law of my God is perfect. It condemns but forgives. It restores—more than abundantly— what it takes away.
Jim Elliot

I had my own experience in which I had lived a servant too long. Ironically, just as my move from believer to servant began in a car ride, in a way, so did my transformation to becoming a friend to Jesus. As I have said before, for about ten years I lived in Chicago. It is a city I deeply love with my Chicago Cubs (yes, I am a glutton for punishment), the lakeshore, its unique architecture, and deep-dish pizza. While living there a couple of years after college, I was now a couple years in my first "official" job. I worked for a large catalog company as a print and paper buyer and loved my job with all of its perks. I often ate at some of the best restaurants, got to see Michael Jordan play on many occasions, and because of my position, I was schmoozed on a regular basis by the other companies that I worked with on the different projects I oversaw.

However, a couple of negative things were also happening, especially in my relationship with God and in my personal life. First, I was becoming callous in my faith and jaded. I had been a Christian for some years, had moved into various places of leadership and was beginning to like that spotlight. In my early years as a Christian I threw myself into many endeavors and slowly but surely was getting burned out and basically, becoming tired of being a Christian. I was leading Bible studies; mentoring a couple of rambunctious seventh graders through Big Brothers; trying to get off the ground a college ministry at the school I graduated from; attending not one, but three different churches. You name it, I was doing it. The problem was…I also trying to keep up appearances, because what once seemingly was a thriving faith had deteriorated. And here was the big problem—the problem was that if you knew me then you would have never known that by looking at all that I was doing. You would have thought I was this great guy who had it all together, serving God and serving others. How do I know this? Because at that time so many around me told me this in not so many words. I had become a very gifted actor and was fit to be the next Robert De Niro.

And underneath all of this, issues from my past had surfaced and secret sins began to pile up. On the surface everything looked like it was in working order, but inside I was hollow and there were so many problems in my life that I wasn't recognizing. First, I was beginning to grow an anger within myself that seemingly just showed up one day. I was hard to please. I was putting high expectations on others, but rarely myself. While up to that point in my life, anger had never really been a struggle or problem, however, now inside I was seething. I often would walk around just a bundle of annoyance and chagrin. I almost never showed this to others, but inside anger had taken a foothold in my life. Second, I had become very arrogant and prideful. I would go to church and not listen to the sermon for self-reflection, but to critique what was being spoken. With others, when someone would have an opinion on some given issue, I often had to disagree. Being a Christian had turned into for me an intellectual exercise and not a spiritual one. *That's not how you interpret that passage! Boy, was that sermon boring! That's not what Jesus meant when he said "Love your enemies!"* Because I had been a Christian for some years, I was slowly becoming a know-it-all and if someone disagreed with me, I could almost in every occasion convince them otherwise. At that time, I learned this—sadly, rarely do people ask tough questions of their leaders.

To top this off, while I had lots of friends, I was distancing myself from them—I carefully hid who I was becoming and where I was struggling. In particular, there was one part of my life which was unraveling and was revealing my brokenness at its deepest levels—its roots, which were nearly twenty years old. Through various experiences in my childhood that had happened to me, some which we would now name as sexual abuse, my sexuality had become an intricate and acute wounded part of me. Like so many that I have met in my practice and in my role as a pastor, my sexuality had been opened up way before it should have been, and with this, the damage that was done was coming to bear. Over the years, in particular starting in my late teenage years, but especially in my early twenties, I was slowly developing a dependency on unhealthy relationships, specifically those that turned sexual.

This brokenness originated at some of my first memories. I became promiscuous at an early age, in part because of these childhood experiences that I mentioned earlier. Likewise, while in middle school, the door had been abruptly slammed open with some incidents with a high school girl who lived down the street and who was a couple of years my senior. We would sneak away to secret places during the summer nights of my eighth grade year and she opened up a world to me that was intoxicating and dangerously mysterious. As I have told many, pornography for the most part has never been a strong urge for me, primarily because of these early experiences. I did not yearn for virtual experiences; I wanted the ones that had flesh and warmth associated with them. These sexual cravings took hold of me at a very early age and would follow for me years to come.

Toward the end of my high school years, this solidified in an even more damaging way—in my freshman year in college, a woman in her twenties who was very "experienced," entirely opened up that part of my life introducing me to a world which I had not quite imagined. Up to that point, for all intents and purposes, I had been dabbling with sex and in this relationship I gave in full blown to my desires. And of course, by no means was I an innocent bystander in all of this—I was enthralled with this lifestyle and at that same time, could not see its dangers.

As I mentioned in an earlier chapter, in my early twenties, I was out of control and did not have the capacity, knowledge or courage to stop what I was doing. I had recently become a Christian, but this transformation had yet to invade my relationships with women. While I might have been having lots of sex, in truth, I was beginning to lose my sexuality and in some way, was losing my capacity to love a woman. I wouldn't of course understand this for years to come, but the ground work had been laid. In these years, I was in many relationships with women, most were just based on having both of our sexual needs met. There were a handful of Saturday mornings that I would awaken next to a woman at my side and I would lay there in a tremendous amount of guilt and shame because of this dual life I was living. The wounds from my sexual past had finally caught up with me, but I did not know what to do.

At about age twenty three, I realized I had to somehow try to get things in respectable order. The problem was I did all this on my own, trying to piece together something that would bring some semblance of wellbeing. For the next couple of years, I managed to keep things together, but only barely. It was at this point where I re-committed my life to God which I detailed in the last section. I seriously dated a couple of women and was trying to take my faith more seriously as well. With the couple of committed relationships that I did have in those years, on the surface they seemed like they were healthy relationships, but in reality, we were two people who had not wrestled with the demons of our past and present. Often in these relationships, I was the overly dependent one and in reality these relationships were becoming a substitute for my relationship with God. I knew I had a serious problem when one Sunday I was standing next to my girlfriend at church and in seeing her in worship; I became jealous of her love toward God. Can you imagine that? I was jealous of God! I remember feeling that emotion and thinking he was going to strike me dead at that very instance. At that point, I knew things were really bad and that what I was trying to do was bringing very little healing to my life.

It all culminated one night at my girlfriend's apartment, in which, in too many words, we had another great argument about our relationship. That evening, we both decided to mutually break things off and that was the beginning for me in pursuing my own healing and relinquishing my craving for women to make me happy and whole. Relieved and devastated at the same time, that evening as I was driving home in my car, I heard a whisper of a voice, which to paraphrase, simply said, *You need to get some help.* Jesus was crying out for me to pursue healing instead of relationships, and soon I was about to finally relent. Remarkably, Jesus was going to begin to heal me in a way that was about as strange as when he used mud and spit to make a blind man see.

HEARING THE UNEXPECTED

If you live in Chicago, you know that you naturally spend a lot of time in your car because of traffic and getting from Point A to Point B. On these stop-and-go drives, I usually listened to Chicago sports radio. The Bulls were winning championships left and right and it was fun listening to the banter about the pride and joy of our city. If you know me, you know that I am not a regular listener to Christian radio or television. However, that night for some reason I turned the dial to some Christian radio station being piped in from one of the suburbs. That night driving down Roosevelt Avenue lonely and sad, I inadvertently came across Bob George's *People to People* radio program. If you have ever listened to Bob George or read his books you know that he talks about one thing over and over at great length—God's grace. For the first time, as I was listening to his words, God began showing me a grace I had not seen before—one that I actually began to experience. In that car ride, listening to his Southern twang talk about acceptance, it opened up my eyes like never before. It was as if Jesus mixed some mud together, rubbed it on my eyes and then commanded me to open them. A couple of days later I grabbed Bob George's book *Growing in Grace* off the bookshelf at a store and took it home. I read it in one sitting and in that time came across this passage below:

> Now realize that I am talking about ourselves being acceptable to God, not necessarily our actions. In my identity I am eternally acceptable to Him, but that doesn't mean that everything I do is all right. He may put His arm around me, so to speak, and show me the truth about something in my life that is out of line: an attitude, action, or habit. Why? So He can change my attitude that is out of line, resulting in a change of action. But at no time is His acceptance of me ever in question.

But at no time is His acceptance of me ever in question. This was one of the missing pieces for me. I knew something like this in concept, but had yet to experience it. Now I began to do that or as the psychologists term, I began to internalize this truth.

During that period in my life, Jesus was also saying that some significant changes needed to occur in my life so that I could really begin to understand that freedom he desired for me. At that point, I made a commitment to not date anyone, even casually. Likewise, I decided I needed to pursue friendships with men, which for the most part was a bit of a challenge for me. Hanging out with women even from a young age was easier for me and for the most part, I enjoyed their company more than hanging out with the guys. However, I began to see that this on some level was contributing to my problem with having healthy relationships with women. With this decision, not until years later did I realize that in this time of healing for me, as I was pursing my relationship with God, I was also pursuing healing in terms of what it meant to be a man. I also decided to remove myself from any ministry context and began reading voraciously books on sexual healing. Specifically, the works of Walter Trobisch had a tremendous influence on me; his books speak openly about sexual issues from a Christian perspective and address certain issues that most books written at that time wouldn't touch with a ten foot pole. Jesus, no different than with Peter, had flipped my world upside down and it was an amazingly lonely, but healing time in my life. In essence, with all that he was doing in my life, he was saying that I had all this focus on ministering to others, but that I had gotten the cart before the horse, and that first, he needed to minister to me. Something, for the most part, I had never allowed him to do.

Ironically, at the end of the day, the main way in which Jesus dealt with me in this healing in terms of all these relational and sexual issues was that he simply forgave me and just as importantly, taught me how to forgive myself. Strangely, these were the two key components that began to change my behavior. Yes, I was reading books, seeking counsel, and doing a myriad of other things to attempt to bring change to my life, but it was these two pieces that began to transform me—His forgiveness and my own forgiveness toward myself. I, for the first time in my life, had truly experienced forgiveness beyond just knowing it in text-book fashion and in word only.

In particular, I can remember one day when I was reading the Bible, God through His words basically said, *Buddy, there are a lot of other areas of your life that you pay little attention to that need even more change than just this area of lust.* I remember that moment because it struck me that I began to see that in some ways the sin of pride was just as damaging to myself and to others as what my sexual sin could be. This was a freeing moment for me. It made me realize how focused I was on this one area of my life, but was neglecting so many others. Again, God was teaching me in a way only that he could, that I was a sinner through and through to the very core. Through this relinquishment, not only did I begin to heal, but I miraculously began to change. The beauty of this time, now that I look back at it now, was that even though I was in this completely broken state, Jesus was extremely patient with me and slowly, but surely was in the process of changing me for the better.

ARE YOU STUCK IN YOUR FAITH?

For those caught in the servant stage of faith, they are often serious about their walk with God. They can remember a distinct time in which they gave their life to Christ and kept that commitment. They attend church regularly. They most likely read their Bible regularly, perhaps repeatedly in the morning or at a meal. They most likely serve in many ways and often. But with all this, something just isn't right. Are you stuck in your faith and living just as God's servant, but not as his friend? Honestly delve deep and ask yourself these questions:

- Typically those who are caught in the servant stage of faith are broken people who have been Christians for awhile, but have not sought healing and growth in specific areas of their lives. Have you genuinely dealt with your brokenness? Are there personal problems (e.g., anger, sexual or emotional issues, over/under eating, bitterness, a wounded past, continued broken relationships, etc.) standing in between you and an intimate relationship with God and with others? Are there some issues in your life that you really need to face but you are afraid to do so? How is your life overall? Is your life in shambles and you have multitudes of secrets and sin? Does your marriage or personal life need work, but you are too proud or afraid to get help because others think you have it all-together and they might not think so highly of you anymore?
- Do you really believe you have it all down pat: your theology, doctrine, who God is, who people are? When someone challenges you on an issue of faith, do you get defensive and do not genuinely listen to them? In conversations like these, do you think the other person is always wrong? After listening to a message or reading a book, do you first and foremost scrutinize what was

said and what was wrong about it rather than humbly applying what you learned to your life? At the end of the day, is your relationship with God just a bunch of head knowledge?

- You might have a lot of Christian friends, but how close do you get to them? Who knows your secrets and do you let people in? If you had to write down the darkest sins of your life, who know about them? Anyone? Not even your spouse?
- Is the basis of your relationship with God based on what you know, but not what you have experienced? Do you have a growing relationship with God or do you just know a lot *about* him? Perhaps you have grown up in the church, but never made your faith your own? Do you know a lot about the Bible, but there's not much of a connection in terms of experience and relationship with him? Again, is your relationship with God just based on knowledge about him or the Bible? As I wrote about in an earlier chapter, *Does Jesus know you*?
- Do you feel close to God when you are obeying all the rules for your life, but when you break them, he feels distant? Does your relationship with God live or die by how you live day-to-day? When you feel like you live "sin-free" for a day (no one does by the way), do you feel closer to God? When you have a rough day and are confronted by your sin, does God then seem distant? If so, you may be stuck in this stage of faith.
- Are you a hard person to be with because you put a lot of do's and don'ts on others? Does everything have to be controlled? And with that, is anger and rage always simmering just underneath the surface toward others? How easy are you to be with? Are you fun to be with or is it a chore to hang out with you? When you look back at your life and your friendships is there a long string of broken relationships?
- More often than not, do the people closest to you think that you

are never satisfied? That when they are with you, that you always have to be in control and do everything "your way?"
- Often are closest relationships reveal the intimacy of our relationship with God. As Jesus said, if you can't do earthly things however would you expect to be able to do heavenly things. (John 3:12) How close are you to your spouse in your marriage and how strong is that relationship? If we asked your children (teenagers and adult) this question how would they respond: how close are you with them to the point that they want to spend time with you—that they truly enjoy your company and don't spend time with you just out of obligation? Do you genuinely love them on a regular basis or is the relationship held up just by control, manipulation and obligation?
- Have you become the Savior for other people? Do you think that you can help everyone around you? Do you spend just as much time working on your own life as you do helping others?
- Really think about this next question—God might love you, but does He like you? When you picture him, is he simply a stern and mean father or does he genuinely care about you and genuinely likes you?
- Those caught in the servant stage of faith do not typically have an intimate relationship with God (they base their faith on what they do) and therefore worship is uncomfortable for them. Do you genuinely like to worship or does it most of the time make you uncomfortable? Do you worship when no one is watching and sing on your own (on the way to work, in the shower, etc.)? Could you do without worship during a church service? Do you really enter into the worship experience or are you most of the time simply going through the motions? Are you just singing words or truly singing and worshipping God?
- Do you really know God's love personally? Is Jesus your Lord,

but to call him your friend would be totally alien to you? Does it seem sacrilegious to you that you would call Jesus your friend?

Part Four

Moving into Friendship with God

THE FRIEND OF GOD - BARNABAS

A fictitious letter written from the hand of John Mark, c. 61 AD
(Acts 15)

Yesterday, my good friend, our good friend, was taken from us. I write this letter with great sadness as our friend, Barnabas was taken outside the city gates of Salamis, and cruel men took him and stoned him. Barnabas had been preaching in that city about the good life of Jesus Christ and a group of men from the synagogue in that town accused him of blasphemy. Without even a trial, they stormed into the home where he was staying, and before daybreak, pulled him out of bed, not even giving him a chance to put his proper garments on and set him before the council in Salamis. Reminiscent of our Savior's trial, they would barely let him get a word out and when he tried, they would strike him with a strong fist to the face. Not much else is known after this incident of the trial. They imprisoned him for two days, and then they must have secretly took him outside the city gates and murdered him there. I have heard from others that many inhumane tortures were done to him prior to the stoning. Three days hence, a traveler found his body and brought it back to the city. This man had found him with his face nearly unrecognizable. The only reason they were able to identify his body was because lying next to his body were some of the writings of Matthew that Barnabas had re-written with his own hand. There in Salamis, that small fellowship gave him a proper burial. My heart is broken because my friend is gone.

As I sit here and write, I remember so many good things he did for so many. Barnabas was unlike most men. He was generous and had a tremendous amount of wealth, but he shared equally with all. I do not know much about where he came from—I know that he was born into a wealthy family and would often sell a piece of property or offer a generous gift to someone who was in need. If you asked something of Barnabas, you always received. And he was a person whose word was always true; when he said he would do something for you he would do it whether that meant sharing the Scriptures with you or even one time, I remember, one of the women in our fellowship had been sick for many days, and he went and tended to her children and her chores for those days.

Barnabas greatly loved children. He was a giant of a man and gentle and you would often find children hung around his big back as he gave them rides as if he was a horse! He loved to be around children, sometimes even more with them then with others. When we had a gathering, and after the Lord's supper had been shared, we would often not be able to find him. After looking for a while, he would be outside and we would find him playing some game with a handful of children.

Of course, I will never forget him, because in many ways he saved my own life. I had joined Paul and Barnabas on a missionary trip—really I was too young, but I thought I knew everything and that I was invincible. We entered the town of Perga and even after a day we began to be ridiculed because of our message about Jesus. I grew very timid. To be frank, I was terrified. What would they do to us? Both of them had told me stories of others who shared the gospel and then were beaten or thrown into jail, but I guess I just didn't really believe that really happened. When a large group of people had surrounded us and were threatening our lives, my knees grew weak and I vomited all over myself. That seemed to calm the crowd down as they laughed at my misfortune, but for me, it opened my eyes and I grew very frightened. I wanted to go back home—I didn't want to continue and so I abandoned them both.

It was over six months later that I saw both of them back in Jerusalem. By this time I had felt awful for what I had done. I had learned of their hard work and the dangers that they had faced. I carry tremendous guilt because really I had not deserted them as much as I had forsaken my Lord. I resolved I would never do such a thing as that again. It was a couple months later and Barnabas and Paul had decided to venture again to Cyprus. I wanted so much to show both of them that I could be trusted and so I went to Antioch and asked if I could join them. Paul immediately barked at me that he would never let me go with him again. He reiterated over and over that I had failed them both in my cowardice. I not only jeopardized my own life, but theirs as well. Paul was furious with me for even bringing it up. Barnabas was trying to calm him down with his big and gentle voice, but Paul's strong words continued and he maintained that he would never let me join them again.

I remember that day well. Barnabas stared at me. He focused on my face and we locked eyes. Admittedly, it was as if I was in Perga all over again and I was frightened. Why was he staring at me so fiercely? As he looked at me, his eyes glistened with tears and he turned to Paul and spoke words that I will never forget and ones that haunt me still.

"Paul, perhaps you have given up on John Mark, but I have not. You take Silas and go to Tarsus. John Mark and I will journey back to Cyprus."

That was it; that was all he said. But his words were solid and strong. I had never heard him speak with such forcefulness and with such conviction. Paul did not say a word, he just nodded twice and as he left the room, he placed his right hand on Barnabas' shoulder. His eyes too began to moisten, because he knew that he would never see his friend again.

As we left, we did not speak for a good hour. I knew I needed to give Barnabas some room to think. Now that I much older, I have learned that even though it is good to make sacrifices, it does not take away the sharpness of the pain. I had cost Barnabas his friend and in that silence I seemed to hear him say that it was okay, not maybe good, but okay.

Barnabas was a good man, easy to be with even when you were difficult. Through him, for the first time I genuinely was learning forgiveness. Not until now do I understand what that was. I did not deserve a second chance. But forgiveness was at hand, and I accepted it. Because of that, I found the courage to sail to Cyprus the following day. Because of that man, I found the courage to follow Jesus and for the first time.

WHEN GOD TEACHES YOU A LESSON LIKE NEVER BEFORE

Then Jesus told them, "This very night you will all fall away on account of me, for it is written: "'I will strike the shepherd, and the sheep of the flock will be scattered.' But after I have risen, I will go ahead of you into Galilee."

Peter replied, "Even if all fall away on account of you, I never will."

"Truly I tell you," Jesus answered, "this very night, before the rooster crows, you will disown me three times." But Peter declared, "Even if I have to die with you, I will never disown you." (Matthew 26:31-35)

Now Peter was sitting out in the courtyard, and a servant girl came to him. "You also were with Jesus of Galilee," she said. But he denied it before them all. "I don't know what you're talking about," he said.

Then he went out to the gateway, where another servant girl saw him and said to the people there, "This fellow was with Jesus of Nazareth." He denied it again, with an oath: "I don't know the man!"

After a little while, those standing there went up to Peter and said, "Surely you are one of them; your accent gives you away." Then he began to call down curses, and he swore to them, "I don't know the man!"

Immediately a rooster crowed. Then Peter remembered the word Jesus had spoken: "Before the rooster crows, you will disown me three times." And he went outside and wept bitterly.

(Matthew 26: 69-75)

As mentioned in the previous chapters, Peter was the quintessential servant. He knew all of the rules by heart, followed them close, and yet missed the point entirely. In fact, it almost cost him his life. When you turn the page from the final chapter of the Gospel of John and flip over into the book of Acts and begin to read about his life, you are seeing the beginnings of what it means to move from a servant of Jesus to being his friend.

When you read the four gospels as a whole and find the different stories about Peter, you will notice a hard man. A man who puts a lot of expectations on others, but very little on himself. A man who points the finger at others, but is not willing to point it back at himself. A man who has all the answers, but really knows very little. In the end, the man we meet in the gospels is not a man who has experienced genuine forgiveness and love. For example, prior to when he denies Jesus those infamous three times, he believes he is going to stand firm next to his Savior and be unafraid of whatever may come. Most definitely, he will stand up to be counted as one of Jesus "servants"—no matter what the cost. But we all know what happens in that courtyard, don't we? He fails Jesus miserably. At that moment in time, he was not a follower of Jesus at all and his Friend was about to teach him a lesson like no other.

Again, Peter in the gospels is the perfect servant and disciple. Go and find a concordance and read all of the different instances in which you find Peter talked about in either the gospel of Mark, Matthew, Luke or John and in eighty percent of those passages, he will come out looking like a heel or worse. No doubt about it, Peter was devoted to Jesus tremendously. In comparison to the other disciples, he was more passionate about following Jesus than any other. He was the one who always had his hand raised first—I picture him like the first grader who is bouncing out of his seat, yelling, "Call on me, Jesus! Call on me, Jesus!" No arguing here, Peter was a very dedicated man, and yet there was also something missing. He had tremendous potential, but it was only potential nonetheless. Jesus had a lot to work with in Peter, but he also had a lot of work to do in him before he could send him out into the world.

And so with all of this, Peter had a couple significant marking points in his life, which thankfully turned everything around. They happened in an upper room, a courtyard and eventually, over a breakfast meal on the beach. But first, let's go back to that story mentioned earlier in a previous chapter. As you will remember, at one point in Peter's life, he emphatically told Jesus that he would always be at his side, through thick and thin. No matter what, even if it meant death, he would never deny knowing his Lord. He would stand with Jesus even if it cost him his life. Even if it meant being crucified right next to him on Golgotha, Peter was never going to fail Jesus. Peter remembered Jesus' rule very well—"if you deny me before men, I will deny you before the Father as well." (Matthew 10:33) In some ways, this was the one rule you should never break and if you broke it, you would be forever lost. Jesus never made such a strong statement about allegiance and if you broke this one, you were going to be sitting on the outside. Peter must have thought to himself, I can never break that one rule. Never! This was one tenet that Peter was never going to break. Or so he thought.

In that scene at the Last Supper, Jesus told Peter in stark and honest terms what was really going to go down—not only once, or twice, but on three separate occasions—Peter was going to act like he never knew Jesus at all. In that moment when Peter again comes back and demands that he will always be loyal, you can picture Jesus rolling his eyes and shaking his head: Peter, Peter, Peter…how wrong you are. The stage is set and in that scene, Peter does two unbelievable things after Jesus challenges him. First, he has the audacity to talk back to Jesus, essentially telling him he had it all wrong. Can you imagine that? Telling the God of the universe that he is wrong?! On top of that, Peter also puts himself above all of the other disciples. He interrupts and equivocally states, "Even if all fall away on account of you, I never will." He's basically saying, these guys aren't trustworthy, but I am. In both instances, he reveals his arrogance and pride. But we all know what happens—everyone knows the end of that story. Again, Peter totally fails and as usual, Jesus was right after all. It all went down just like Jesus said.

And then after everything happened as Jesus foretold concerning his death and resurrection, Peter could not be found. Jesus hangs out with Mary Magdalene, Cleopas and even the ever-doubting Thomas. Peter knew what he had done and perhaps he thought that it was all over for him. Peter knew full well Jesus' words about the consequences of betraying him. I am sure he had heard of the news of Judas' death and suicide. It was looking about as bleak for him as well. Did Peter perhaps have fleeting thoughts of taking his own life as well? Peter, in the back of his mind could see how Jesus was going to react to him—Peter, you know what I said and you know the rules and consequences. Now get away from me, because you failed me. This is exactly why Peter wasn't very eager to see Jesus even though he had heard stories about his amazing return. If you really mull this over, Peter was no different than Judas—he was a traitor too. There was no good news in that story for Peter, because he knew what the outcome would be. It was all over for him. Isn't that how the story ends? If you fail your friend, your friend fails you? Listen to how this section of the story ends: "Peter went out and wept bitterly." (Matthew 26:75) What a tremendously sad scene. On so many levels for Peter it was a very sad day indeed. Again, is this how the story ends?

HOW HAVING BREAKFAST WITH JESUS CAN CHANGE YOUR LIFE

When they had finished eating, Jesus said to Simon Peter, "Simon son of John, do you love me more than these?"

"Yes, Lord," he said, "you know that I love you."

Jesus said, "Feed my lambs."

Again Jesus said, "Simon son of John, do you love me?"

He answered, "Yes, Lord, you know that I love you."

Jesus said, "Take care of my sheep."

The third time he said to him, "Simon son of John, do you love me?"

Peter was hurt because Jesus asked him the third time, "Do you love me?" He said, "Lord, you know all things; you know that I love you."
(John 21:15-19)

But again and again, Jesus writes a different story and makes a different way out for us—a way of forgiveness, mercy and grace. One day, Jesus decides to go hunt Peter down and rescue him from himself. Where would he find him—fishing early in the morning and back at his old job. As he calls him to come out of the boat and join him for some breakfast, perhaps one of the more riveting stories in all of Scripture unfolds.

In this story, it's a very simple one. In your Bible, the section is often entitled *Jesus Reinstates Peter* or something similar. I think a better title would be *Peter Finally Learns Grace* with a strong emphasis on the word "finally." Remember, Jesus clearly said earlier that if anyone were to deny him before anyone, he would forsake them also. This is exactly why Peter was not very eager to catch up with Jesus after the resurrection. Peter believes he has just ruined his entire life. He knows what Jesus said and now he has to live by those words. But this shows you just how much Jesus is willing to forgive and just how great his mercy can be.

When reading an English translation of the Bible with the scene above, it does not do a good job of capturing the words and the actual conversation that is taking place between Jesus and Peter. Almost every Bible written in English has a difficult time in translating these verses because unlike the Greek language, we only have one word for love. So with this, before one reads this passage, you need to have an understanding of the Greek words for love. In the passage above, it is using two unique and different words for love. Let's look at a couple of these Greek words.

First, one word that is used for love in this passage is the word *agape*, which in layman's terms simply means godly love. *Agape* is a rich word and is comprised of many facets to its meaning. In one example, it is derived from the word love-feast, which we might think of the word for us as being communion—a very intimate fellowship. Likewise, this type of love is highly sacrificial; it's a love that is long-suffering; it's a love that is best exemplified by the cross. One description states that it means to "to be well pleased, to be contented at or with something." I like that description because that is Jesus' love toward us and a love that he wants for us to have toward ourselves and toward others. He wants us to know that he is well-pleased and contented with us. It's the type of love which Jesus is attempting to develop in each of us, because in no way shape or form do we have the ability to experience this love naturally toward ourselves or to others. This love is supernatural. And this is the final and most unique thing about this love—it can only occur by being in a relationship with Jesus.

Only those who have a relationship with God can acquire this love no matter how hard they try. It's inevitably connected up with having a relationship with Jesus. Twice in the Bible, it puts it as simple as it can be said: God is *agape* (I John 4:8, 16). However, the other two loves found in the Scriptures are more natural and for a better word, lesser to a degree in comparison to this type of love. As C.S. Lewis wrote in his book *The Four Loves*, *agape* is the highest level of love—it is the one which is the standard. It is the coup de gris. At the end of the day, it's the one you want to be holding.

Anybody can experience these other types of loves that we will now discuss. They are fairly common and the ones we most think of when we think of the word love. They are open to anyone and anyone can tap into them. In most relationships, these are the ones that are at work. These are the lesser loves. First, another Greek word for love is *phileo*; it simply means friendship. On one level, this is a love in which you care for the person and have similar interests. The word Philadelphia is derived from this word, which we know as the city of brotherly love. That's a good way to put it. However, with this have you ever seen two brothers together? It can sometimes be a love-hate relationship. It's either on or it's not. *Phileo* can be a deep love, but it can also be shallow. Aristotle in his book *Nicomachean Ethics* spends a great deal of time talking about this word *phileo*. One section captures the essence of this type of love; in describing it, he gave an example of the type of friendship, such as between "a cobbler and the person who buys from him." Now that isn't a very deep love, is it? *Phileo* can be as deep as the love you have for the person who checks out your milk and eggs at the grocery store? Aristotle also went on to say that *phileo* was based on friendships of utility, meaning a love in which you expect to get something out of the relationship. In that sense, *phileo* is a selfish love—what are you going to do for me. As you can see, it can be a love that doesn't go terribly deep and is amuck with some troubling aspects. Remember this type of love, we will be coming back to it and look at it further.

The other word for love in the Greek is *eros*—it's passionate or physical love. Sexual love is the most common way we think about the word *eros*; but this type of love is not only erotic in nature. It can be holding hands at a movie or when you look at someone with wow in your eyes. It can be passion, zeal, excitement, lust and infatuation all rolled up in one. Like the love *phileo*, it also can be fleeting and not terribly stable. Again, it's a love that is necessary and important to our lives, but in the long run, it's not a love that over the long haul is something solid or secure.

WHEN PETER'S LIFE TURNED ON A DIME

Now let's go back to the passage where Jesus is on the beach and calling out to Peter to come to him and have a conversation with him over breakfast. Here, Jesus when using the words for love is using both the words *agape* and *phileo*. It is important to look at the questions Jesus asks and also listen to Peter's answers. Here is how the Greek reads: Jesus first asks, "Peter, do you *agape* me?" But Peter doesn't answer that question—he responds differently and answers, "No, Jesus I *phileo* you." Again, Jesus puts the question back to him, "Peter, do you *agape* me?" Again, Peter seems to evade the real question and answers it just as before. "No, Jesus, I *phileo* you." Finally on the third try, this then becomes the most beautiful part of the whole passage, because now Jesus asks Peter a different question—"Peter, do you *phileo* me?"

Why does Jesus do this? Why is this so important? Jesus knows full well that Peter does not and has never up to that point loved him with this *agape* love. Jesus knows full well that Peter has never genuinely loved him. If we were to translate this scene in a way that captures what is really happening between the both of them, it might read something like this:

> Jesus: Peter, do you truly love me with all your heart and with every inch of your being?
>
> Peter: No, Lord, I only kind of love you, just a little bit, but really not very much.

In our English language, these nuances are difficult to capture. This is the exchange between them with Jesus' first two questions and then with Jesus' final question, he really is asking: "Peter, do you kind of love me? But not really?" This is *phileo* love and the question Jesus really wants to ask. And then Peter does the most remarkable thing, he finally speaks the truth a third time, "Yep, that's true, Lord, I only kind of love you, but not really."

This is a major breakthrough for Peter, because previously he would have demanded over and over, *Yes, Jesus, of course, I agape you! Haven't I proved that night and day!* The problem would have been that he wouldn't have been speaking the truth. Now Peter tells it like it is. He's honest with Jesus and just as importantly, with himself. So much so that as we venture into the stories in the book of Acts, Peter just a few short days later, truly begins to *agape* Jesus for the first time. It is a remarkable transformation and it all occurred because of Jesus' grace and forgiveness and then Peter's acceptance of himself and the acceptance of that gift.

The passage has a beauty to it, because on the one hand, Jesus is testing Peter. But on the other hand, at the same time, he is lowering Peter's expectations of himself and is teaching Peter the basics of forgiving himself. At the heart of it, yes, Jesus wants Peter to have this *agape* love for him; he knows that would be the best for Peter, because again *agape* love is more solid and strong than other types of love. It's not fleeting such as what Peter experienced in the courtyard when he denied Jesus those three times. Essentially, Jesus is saying, *Peter, I want you to agape me, but for now, this love of phileo you have for me will do.* Again, there are many ways in which we can love God; what Jesus is instilling in Peter is that in reality his love for him previous to all of this was flat and one-dimensional. The love of *agape* is three-dimensional—full of communion and intimacy and can only come at the cost of forgiveness and grace—first, for yourself and then for others. This is the point that Jesus was making. He knew first-hand Peter's arrogance and pride, but he broke those traits through the remarkable transformation of grace and forgiveness which eventually changed him in a way he never expected.

This is the turning point in Peter's life. It wasn't when his brother Andrew introduced him to Jesus three years prior. This is Peter's genuine "born again" experience; this is when he truly began to follow Jesus. Again, compare Peter in the gospels and then go read his letters that we find in the New Testament, which he wrote in the years following this incident. You will see a marked difference. He is gentle, kind and patient and it's as if when reading these words in First and Second Peter, you are encountering an entirely different man. This is exactly what needs to happen to each of us. This is the first step toward a friendship with God. The last words Peter wrote in his second book say it all and exemplify the transformation he underwent: "But grow in the grace and knowledge of our Lord and Savior Jesus Christ. To him be the glory both now and forever. Amen." (2 Peter 3:18) Peter's challenge with these words came because of first-hand experience—to know his grace and to know that Jesus is easy to live with.

Just as we have looked at different persons from Scripture like Judas and Peter to exemplify the different roles of believer and servant, here we can look to John as our model as the friend of Jesus. John was the perfect friend of Jesus. I love the books John wrote. The gospel of

THE END OF ALL OUR EXPLORING

John is by far my favorite book because of how he wrote it. John was poetic, apocalyptic, a wonderful storyteller. However, the most important aspect of his book which clearly comes out is that he had a strangely close relationship to Jesus. John was a friend of Jesus. Even how John refers to himself in his books is at first almost startling. Without embarrassment, without blinking an eye, with great pride—John often refers to himself as "the one Jesus loved." Even as I am writing these words now—"the one Jesus loved"—it brings tears to my eyes as I realize that's how Jesus wants each of us to relate to him. *You are the one who Jesus loves.* When you understand that at its core, you have met that place which is the most important starting point of your life. You have become Jesus' friend.

In the gospel of John, Jesus insists, "No longer do I call you servants, but now I call you friend." I can be, you can be, no longer a servant, but a friend of the One who created the beluga whale, the vastness of the Rocky Mountains, the planet Saturn. This is pretty amazing stuff. He says to you that you are his center point; his focus; his all in all. Dwell on that. Think about that. No longer do I call you servants but now I call you friend. This is the Creator of the world talking to you—directly to you.

How does that happen? How does one get to the point of being the friend of Jesus? How does one get to this place? In a way I've got some really bad news and that is I believe that for each person, it is a unique experience. It's personal. Like in all things it's a matter of grace and at the same time, our attempt to knock on some doors. God makes it happen, and yet you must make it happen in your life as well. I can share with you my own experience and I can explain some details about of those who have followed a similar path, but your journey will be unique —with some similarities to mine, but also with some differences as well. However, in saying that, I do believe that there are some essential building blocks that need to be put in place before you can know how to refer to yourself as "the one Jesus loves." In the up-coming chapters we will look at some of these necessary ingredients.

Winston Churchill was quoted as saying that to be successful one has to be audacious. These are my sentiments exactly as it pertains to our relationship with God—we need to be audacious with him. I would say that God wants us to challenge him on so many different levels. Believe it or not, he really does want a relationship with us. And a rich one at that. Just as we make a choice in becoming a believer or servant, we must also make a choice in becoming a friend of God. That's what Peter did on the beach as he ate fish with Jesus. The question you really have to ask yourself and answer it honestly is this—why would God want a relationship with me? Let's explore some ways in which maybe you can be audacious with God.

KNOWING THE TRUTH ABOUT OURSELVES

What looks like a loss may be the very event, which is subsequently responsible for helping to produce the major achievement of your life.
Srully Blotnick

Remembrance of things past is not necessarily the remembrance of things as they were.
Marcel Proust

When all is said and done, there are some necessary steps that we must make to move into a friendship with God. One the one hand, they are daunting steps, no different than when Peter attempted to walk out onto the stormy sea when Jesus called him. And on the other hand, it will be the easiest thing we ever did in our lives, because from the beginning of time, this is where Jesus wanted us all along. In the rest of the book, we will explore what these challenges and changes are so that we can move to that place of friendship with him. While some of this might be scary and we might be unsure of our steps, at the end of the day, they will become some of the most exhilarating moments of our lives.

A crucial first step when one enters into friendship is that we begin to genuinely know and acknowledge who we are—flaws and all. With this, there is an understanding of ourselves in that we know that we are the worst of worst sinners no different than what Paul wrote about himself nearly 2,000 years ago (I Timothy 1:15-16). People like this have an understanding of what sin is like and what sin can do. Those who are moving in step with God know how to handle the sin and brokenness in their lives in healthy ways. Here is an important truth: friends of Jesus understand that they are sinners and they are okay with that, and they are not okay with that. They have the ability to hold those two truths in tension.

As an example, for some people they see things very black and white and they see two different types of sin—bad sin and good sin. What are the bad sins? Typically, these are things like sexual sin, stealing or killing someone. These are the big hitters. However, others like—laziness, gossip, greed, idolatry, arrogance, selfishness, divisiveness, cheating, jealously, being mean—these are the ones that aren't so obvious. These are just to name a few and many see them as the "good" sins or in other words, the ones we typically overlook. There is a bumper sticker I have seen a handful of times on someone's car—it simply reads "Mean People Suck." I laugh every time I see it. I ask myself, doesn't the person who slaps that on their bumper know that they "suck"—that they are mean themselves? Here is a truth—everyone is mean. Everyone says hurtful things; everyone does things that are completely wrong; there isn't a person on earth who shouldn't get used to uttering the words "I'm sorry." It can be so easy to not look in the mirror about our lives, but yet friends of Jesus know how to do this and they do it often.

There isn't a day in which each of us hasn't messed up multiple times in different ways. It is inherent in our very nature and we will never get away from this until the One we follow makes us perfect. The heart is deceitful above all things, this I know to be true (Jeremiah 17:9). I've seen it in my own life and I've seen it countless times with the people that I work with in the sharing of their stories with me. The human person is always struggling to hide. Listen to what the gospel of John says:

> This is the verdict: Light has come into the world, but people loved darkness instead of light because their deeds were evil. Everyone who does evil hates the light, and will not come into the light for fear that their deeds will be exposed. But whoever lives by the truth comes into the light, so that it may be seen plainly that what they have done has been done in the sight of God. (John 3:19-21)

This passage offers what that difference is between the person who follows Jesus in their life and the one who does not. It declares one of chief differences—the one who is following is totally okay with coming into the light about their lives. The other person who isn't following Jesus closely—they are terrified of being exposed of who they really are. It's the father in great rage who beats the tar out of his son with a garden hose on a Saturday afternoon, and yet the next day goes to church with a smile and a "praise the Lord." The wife who in her frustration with her own life turns to another man and tries to find solace in his arms. The young man who secretly pockets cash from customers while the boss goes out to lunch each Tuesday. The young woman who bitterly says false things to friends at school about a teen-age rival. We all have secrets, dark ones and there is this pull in which we want them to stay hidden.

LEARNING TO BE COURAGEOUS

Yet thankfully, on the other hand, there is also a place within each of us that wants them out into the light. Deep within us, each of us wants to be known. The truly courageous let their lives be known for what they truly are. Most of us are terribly afraid to let our dark secrets be known. To be in a relationship to Jesus, one can come to a place where we can be unafraid to be authentic in our walk with God. Some of you who are reading this have terrible secrets, either things done to you or things that you have done. You've never shared these things with anyone and they fester within you. Let's not white wash our situation, we live in a very fallen world and we are good at appearances. Each of us has had some very cruel things done to us and we at the same time have been very cruel to others as well.

Friends of Jesus understand that there are all types of brokenness in their lives and in the lives of those around them. They know that sin is sin is sin. There is not "good" sin and there isn't "bad" sin—all types of sin are really bad and cause havoc in our lives. In general, we need to know that there are two kinds of sins in which we can get caught. They are the sins of omission and commission. The sin of commission is something that we do wrong; we literally by the act of our will do something that God has said we should not do. This is typically what we think of when we think of the word sin. As example, such actions would be things like murder, stealing, adultery and the like. Again, culturally speaking, these are the bad sins.

The sin of omission is not something we typically think of as "sin." Sins of omission are when we fail to do something God wants us to do. An example of this would be if a cashier mistakenly gave me an extra twenty dollar bill in returning my change and I didn't speak up about their mistake. Because I failed to do what I was supposed to do (i.e., share with them their mistake), I "missed the mark," which is the typical description of the word sin. When I was living in Chicago, there was a terrible incident that happened that illustrates these two different types of sin. One morning a woman was on the train platform and waiting for the train. As she was standing there, a man brutally raped and beat her almost to the point of death. Standing there, on the platform with her were nearly twenty people who did not do a thing to stop the incident which lasted nearly ten minutes. This incident is an example of the sins of commission and omission. In this case, both the man and the crowd on the train platform committed tremendous acts of evil. The individuals who sat idly by were just as evil as the person who victimized this woman. From a biblical perspective, on the day that this man stood trial for his crime and was found guilty, each of those twenty individuals should have also faced the same punishment.

However, in our day and age, the mere word sin is seemingly medieval, unnecessary and politically incorrect. Overall, we have forgotten who we are and what we are capable of. It can be good to go back to the ancient and medieval Christians who took the act of sin very seriously and had a detailed description and outline for it. As an example, the ancient fathers appropriately saw sin in various and vast ways. One could be sinful if they had:

- Excessive love of others (lust)
- Over-indulged anything to the point of waste (gluttony)
- Hoarded materials or objects (greed)
- Procrastinated in what you were supposed to be doing (sloth)
- Inappropriately yelled at someone (wrath)
- Wanted something someone else had (envy)
- Thought they were better than someone (pride)

As another example, Thomas Aquinas took an expansive view of sin and categorized six different types of gluttony:

- *Praepropere* - eating too soon
- *Laute* - eating too expensively
- *Nimis* - eating too much
- *Ardenter* - eating too eagerly
- *Studiose* - eating too daintily
- *Forente* - eating wildly

We may look at this list and laugh, but there is something that we can learn in taking sin this seriously. What does sin do—it brings harm and brokenness to our lives, inevitably distances us from God (not the other way round), and can have long-lasting consequences. Why is looking at this so important; why should we be so detailed in addressing the sin and fallenness in our lives? Simply, so that we know where we need to grow. This is precisely what friends of Jesus do in an appropriate and healthy way. They fully look at their lives and address the areas where they fall short. They look at their lives and see how they hurt others and themselves and they do this with great self-examination down to the finest element.

Taking this discussion a step further, we need to also understand the danger of how we inevitably are drawn to hide our sin. Alice Sebold in her book *The Lovely Bones* tells the story of a young girl, Suzie, who at the tender age of twelve is brutally raped and murdered by her neighbor, Mr. Harvey. While in heaven, she is able to look down and see her sister

Lindsey, her father and mother, and friends deal with this horrific incident. Because she is on the other side of the tragedy, she has a wisdom, because she can see the big picture. The novel paints a real and dark picture of how our world can sometimes be—where murder and rape really does happen. By no means is it an easy read. Too often we don't want to see how life really can be, to realistically live in a world that is stained by sin—that little girls are raped and murdered, that fathers do beat their sons; that in our vocabulary, we do have words like rage, genocide, and hatred.

In Sebold's book, there's is a scene in which Suzie meets all the different girls in heaven who her perpetrator, Mr. Harvey has also murdered. She tells us something that is profound and it's something that each of us needs to address in our own lives:

> Our heartache poured into one another like water from cup to cup. Each time I told my story, I lost a bit the smallest drop of pain…Because horror on the earth is real and it is every day. It's like a flower or the sun. It can't be contained.

Each time I told my story. In the next three chapters, we will discuss the importance of doing what Suzie recommends and how we can pursue this for ourselves—how we can open up and share the stories of our lives.

FACING MYSELF

As you get older, you find that often the wheat, disentangling itself from the chaff, comes out to meet you. Gwendolyn Brooks

Man may well change himself; otherwise, he would not be man. Vicktor Frankl

The fundamental human problem is that people are afraid of change. Rei Kawakubo

An important pursuit that is vital to undertake for those who wish to move into friendship with Jesus is a two step process that goes hand in hand: 1) Looking at the real areas of struggle in your life, and 2) Pursuing genuine forgiveness toward yourself and for others. A person has to get real with themselves and move beyond the excuse of "this is just who I am." We have to face head on the shattered parts of our lives and look at the areas where we need to make changes. We each have our problems and secrets in our lives; each of us have the places where we struggle on a day-to-day basis, but if we continue to bury or disguise them, they will create even bigger problems in our lives. We eventually need to come clean about who we are and where we've been and the poor choices we have made in our lives. This is one of the first steps we must make if we want to learn how to move into friendship with Jesus.

The first step in this process has to first begin with self-examination. You can never forgive yourself unless you genuinely know how you have failed. The purpose of this self-examination is to evaluate truthfully what is contributing to the problems in your life, be that personal struggles or in your relationships. Here might be a few questions that you need to ask yourself to begin that journey:

- Why am I always so angry? Or depressed? Or anxious?
- Why has my career stagnated? Or why am I seemingly always in and out of jobs?

- Why do I never finish what I start?
- Why do I care very little about nurturing my relationship with God?
- Why do I have no real friends, those who will be there for me through thick and thin?
- Why has my kid estranged himself from me?
- Why do I always feel like I need a drink? Or to eat? Or to look at porn? Or to shop?
- Why does my spouse always put up a wall to me? Or why do I not want to get close to my spouse emotionally and sexually?
- Why do I always want to stay at work and not go home to my family?

Through honest self-assessment, you can begin to change your thinking and behavior. In terms of how people handle their brokenness in a dysfunctional and unhealthy way, they usually fall into two different camps:

1. They let their brokenness incapacitate their lives, because of the unceasing guilt they feel when they fail. They often respond to this type of guilt in self-harming ways such as through emotional problems, addictions, broken relationships, etc.
2. They deny, ignore or rationalize their brokenness and typically do not experience guilt when they sin. When they do feel guilt, this is usually a momentary response and then it is quickly forgotten.

One of the first psychologists who integrated psychology and spirituality, Roberto Assagioli wrote, "Without forgiveness, life is governed by an endless cycle of resentment and retaliation." These are the two types of people that we just discussed above: the first person is dragged down by the lack of self-forgiveness and the other person continues to hurt others, because they never face their brokenness and their automatic response to sin. For that second person, the one who typically does not experience a guilty conscience, self-forgiveness is not possible, because this person is unwilling to face the fact that they hurt themselves and that they often hurt others. Throughout my life, sadly, I have known many Christians who fall in this camp.

For the first person, the person who "resents" themselves and let's their sin drag them down to depression or a whole other slew of problems, there is hope. For individuals like these, they have a behavior pattern in which they use guilt in a self-perpetuating cycle. For this person, here is how that pattern typically works in an unhealthy way:

1. They do something wrong
2. They feel guilty about what they did
3. They punish themselves in some way (e.g., emotional problems, addictions, broken relationships, etc.).
4. They forget what they did and perhaps hide their failings (i.e., they move to denial).
5. Inevitably, they end up repeating what they did wrong or a variation of it.

This cycle continues because of two important mechanisms. First, it is because we do not take full responsibility for our actions and make real changes in our lives. We do not do the hard things to change. If you ask a lot of people about the areas where they struggle, they want to change in multiple areas of their lives. However, this is where the rubber meets the road—we all know real change requires sacrifice, purpose, and courage. These aspects are what many fail to do—make honest and real change in their lives by taking practical steps.

STEPS IN MAKING LONG-LASTING CHANGE

So how do we start the process of taking responsibility and create change in our lives? First, by considering with complete honesty the part we play in any situation and accepting our role in creating troubles in our lives. Remember those questions I mentioned above—these are the types of questions we need to evaluate in how we have become the problem. Here are a few examples:

- Why don't I ever seem to finish what I start? *Is it because I have a major problem with procrastinating and that I need to practically work on being more disciplined and self-controlled?*
- Why do I have no real friends who will be there for me through thick and thin? *Is it because, to be honest, I am rarely a good friend—a person who can be counted on, who protects confidential conversations, and sacrifices in tangible ways for the other person?*
- Why has my kid estranged himself from me? *Is it because I have a major problem with anger and manipulation, and have never sought to repair that relationship with my son by acknowledging how I have broken the relationship?*

There have been and are many different areas of my own life when I have not dealt with my struggles in this way. Often, it is difficult to look at my life and see what damage I am doing, and what needs mending and change. One major point in my life when this began to happen was when I got married, when Julie entered into my life, and as a mirror, I began to see my brokenness like never before through her eyes. I think in some marriages this initially begins to happen, but then that aspect of accountability is left by the way side for various reasons. Often because of the motivations of fear, laziness or compliance, we relinquish our responsibility to hold our spouse (or friend) accountable for their bad behavior. We begin to overlook their faults and problems—how our spouse is verbally abusive, seemingly lies all the time, cheats on their taxes each year, is inappropriate with those of the opposite sex or are always involved in gossip in some way or other. Some, in these cases, remain silent. However, the truth is that there is no better accountability then when one is married as it is the most intimate of relationships.

As an example, Julie knows better than anyone the great guy I am. But also, Julie knows better than anyone the awful man that I am. If she does not gently, but firmly challenge me, I will never become the man that I was created to be. In most cases, she knows me better than I know myself, because I have so many blind spots and I can so quickly go to rationalizing how I struggle and sin. I am glad she enters my life in this manner even though it isn't always enjoyable or pretty. Is she always right when she challenges me or does this process come without conflict? Absolutely not. But in these tensions and arguments, we are living out the Proverb "As iron sharpens iron, so one person sharpens another." (27:17) This also is what the Scriptures refer to as a "help-mate." This quality also makes me think of a quote by Joseph Barth: "Marriage is our last, best chance to grow up." Marriage can become the catalyst for us to look deeply at our misgivings, misfortunes and sin, but only if both parties are open to being honest, gentle and vocal about helping each other make real and specific change.

SOMETHING TO TRY

To get the ball rolling in looking at your life, below are some things to mull over and then to act on—you should probably take your time and journal out your answers:

- What are the top five places you struggle and be specific. For example, this is how you could write this out if you struggle with anger: *I have outbursts of anger and simply feel angry most of the time. This has led to me harming my children and spouse. Because of my anger, this most likely ties to my struggle with overspending.* Attempt to do an exhaustive list and journal out these areas where you need to seek help from someone. After you have this completed, write out three different things you are going to do to try to heal and mature in these areas. Make sure you add these to a calendar or to-do list so that you pursue them.
- Who are the three people you have trusted the most? What did they do or who were they that you trusted them so much? Name three circumstances in which you had trust broken? Detail these situations above in a journal. Find at least one person to whom you can share these stories.

FACING FORGIVENESS

Man, when he does not grieve, hardly exists.
Antonio Pochia

He who has not forgiven an enemy has not yet tasted one of the most sublime enjoyments of life.
Johann K. Lavater

The second aspect of this process of facing the reality of our lives is learning how to apply forgiveness to your life. As a start, I like what Lily Tomlin said: "Forgiveness means giving up all hope for a better past." I like that because the truth is that I can't change what I've done, be that twenty years ago or just today when I hurt someone close to me with some blunt and harsh words. Yes, I need to take responsibility and then to attempt to change how I am acting, but I can't alter the past and make that ugly event (whatever that was) just disappear and go away. Again, we are sinners through and through, and there is only so much we can do to change that truth.

When forgiving ourselves of the sin that we do, we first have to see it and acknowledge it as we discussed above, but the next part is that you need to forgive yourself and begin to let it go. Earlier I discussed the negative cycle that we can perform—below is how the cycle of sin, guilt and forgiveness should go:

1. We do something wrong.
2. We feel guilty about what we did.
3. We acknowledge what we did to God and ask for his forgiveness.
4. In most cases, we apologize in word and action to the person we wronged. We communicate to them that we will try not to hurt them again in this way.
5. We make active changes to stop this specific failing in our lives.

6. We forgive ourselves of the wrong we have done to God and/or to the person/s we hurt.
7. We relinquish the ability to change ourselves and allow God to help us make these changes.

Let's walk through a living example in my life and discuss this process a bit. Prior to getting married, I was a fairly laid back guy, nothing frustrated me much and emotionally I was usually calm when things got a little tough. This changed noticeably the day I got married, and especially after our sons were born. Almost overnight, I became this Type A person, where everything had to be in its proper place and now even little things began to bother me in dramatic fashion. For the most part my life was stress-free and now the responsibilities of "real life" began to take over and I reacted like a lot of people do. Outbursts of anger became a natural occurrence and became my companion in the way that I would handle tension and troubles. If something was wrong—the dishes hadn't gotten done, money was overspent, my relationship with Julie wasn't what I thought it should be—those closest to me knew my temper too well. Over time, I became very adept with the emotions of anger and rage.

With one occurrence, my sin was exposed in a way which even to remember this event today still reminds me how my brokenness can be so damaging to others. One hectic day which seemingly was busier than most, I backed up our Toyota Sequoia into our garage door, and initially I thought it was my youngest son's fault because of his negligence. In a sudden outburst, I screamed at him like never before. I saw a look of fear and insecurity on his face that is etched in my mind to this day. That was the day I knew things weren't good with me. By looking at his little face, at that moment I saw in clear view what my sin had done and what it could do.

Years earlier if this same incident had occurred, I would not have gone though any of the steps I will now describe. I would have just moved on and a wake of hurt would have been left with that wave of rage that I had poured out onto my son. If I had ignored that moment, that pain would still be evident to this day and I am positive I would not be the same person I am today, nor would my son. I would not have looked in the mirror; I would have either denied I had a problem or ignored it all together. Thankfully, God got my attention and I began to learn how to face my brokenness. This was one of the first days that I genuinely began to deal with my struggle with anger and learn forgiveness in real time. That day, I began to do things differently when I failed myself, my son and God.

LEARNING THE ART OF APOLOGIZE

First, as each of us experiences on a regular basis when we do something wrong—in that moment in the garage, with a major dent in the garage door, I began to feel guilty. I had seen the look on my son's face; I had hurt his five-year old soul deeply and I knew it. At that moment in time, with my bumper sitting squarely against the garage door, my son with his look of insecurity, God whispered a simple yet firm question to me: *So now do you think you have a problem?* In my mind's eye, I simply nodded and in my thoughts I asked for God's grace. This is the first step in the process of forgiveness—I did wrong, I acknowledged it internally, and I asked for God's forgiveness. For most, this step is very easy and one that many are used to—sadly, too many do not go any further than this. For some they can't even see in a circumstance like this that they have done wrong; for others, the mechanics are just internal to themselves and the following steps are ignored. Now for the harder parts.

How do you apologize to a son who is welling up with tears? After seeing my youngest dissolve into tears, I realized that it wasn't his fault at all that I had backed up into our garage door. Because of my own misjudgment, I was really the one to blame; I was the one who had been negligent. This often is the problem with an outburst of anger—in being upset, sometimes the one you should accuse is yourself. I cannot tell you how many times I have gotten angry at someone when in reality, I was the one at fault. It is sadly ironic to say the least. In this instance, as I saw Micah looking at me dumbfounded and not knowing how to respond to a tyrannical madman, I turned off the car, looked him in the eyes and simply said this, *Buddy, will you forgive me for yelling at you? It isn't your fault. It was mine and I am sorry I hurt your feelings by screaming at you. I will try to never yell at you in that way again.* It became one of my first apologies I had ever done to someone other than Julie, and it surprisingly freed my soul. Why? Because in the past I maybe had said I was sorry, but I had not done two additional things. First, I had not said what I was sorry about and most importantly, that I was committed to changing my behavior in the future. Previous to this, I offered generic apologies. In all the years that I have been in private practice or in my work as a pastor, I am astonished at how few people actually say the words "I am sorry" to someone they have wronged. As a Christian, these three words should be a regular part of our vocabulary. But beyond this, it is just as important to not only apologize, but to also follow this up with stating how you will attempt to change as well. I can't tell you how many appointments I have had in which I have explained this crucial aspect of apology and the person across my desk replies, *Really, I have to actually say I am sorry, why I am sorry and that I will try not to do it again?* To begin to experience forgiveness toward yourself, this is one of the essential prerequisites—you not only have to say that you are sorry, but you must also communicate that you will try not to do it again.

MOVING BEYOND JUST SAYING YOU'RE SORRY

But we can't just stop there. Beyond this apology, I had to get help and so I began to make active changes in my life that week. I realized how much I lived a life without peace and how this was a catalyst for my struggle with anger. If a person wants to live differently with the struggles they have, they have to make active and practical changes in their life. This is where the rubber meets the road and is the gigantic difference between the person who makes strides in their personal struggles and those who don't. It's the difference between the person who really changes in the areas they fail and those that don't. The practical changes for me were many, but essentially came down to one specific area that desperately needed modifying. What was this? Through counseling, I learned that I literally had to change how I think. One of the things I had read in the many books that I had poured over about anger was this—*our thinking is integrated into our emotions which eventually leads to how we act.* As the novelist Elizabeth Gilbert penned, "You are, after all, what you think. Your emotions are the slaves to your thoughts, and you are the slave to your emotions." One of the exercises in one of the books that I read detailed that keeping a journal of your thoughts was the first step in not only changing your thinking, but also your emotions and actions. Granted, often what we think about has nothing to do with something we are feeling, but when I tried this, it was amazing to see how often my thoughts revolved around emotions of anger and vice versa. Whether it was thinking about an incident that had happened during the day that had upset me or even just listening to a news program driving on the way home from work, I was astonished how often my thoughts triggered bitter or enraged feelings. This, I had to change—I had to change how I was thinking and where I put my thoughts.

  One of the most effective ways to do this is what psychologist's call *thought-stopping*. The basis of this technique is that you consciously speak a command to yourself to stop the negative and repeated thoughts you are having. The principle behind thought-stopping is fairly simple—by interrupting troublesome thinking, it serves as a reminder and a distraction, especially if you replace that negative thought with a positive one. When using this technique, one can think of I Corinthians in its command to "renew your mind." (2:16) This is what thought-stopping does—you become aware of unhealthy thinking and replace it with helpful thoughts instead of negative ones. As an example, if I was washing the car or sitting at my desk, I would monitor my thoughts and see if there was a negative emotion attached to these thoughts. When I realized that my thinking was pessimistic or antagonistic, I would attempt to stop what I was thinking. While seemingly simple, this change slowly began to help me adjust my thinking, which inevitably began to change how I felt about something. Previous to this "renewing of my mind," I would just let my mind wander and let it go wherever it wanted. By putting an end to this, my thinking began to change, which unmistakably changed my feelings of anger and the regrettable actions that inevitably ensued. I was slowly learning how to become a person of peace.

The final two pieces of this process of facing your junk are connected—we will call these aspects self-forgiveness and relinquishment. On the one hand, if a person is not fully dealing with their failings—acknowledging, apologizing, and actively changing—the first part, self-forgiveness doesn't even come into the equation. If you can get past these crucial pieces, in the grand scheme of things, the final two might be relatively easy. The first part is that you have to forgive yourself of what you did wrong, but you must really believe and live that you are a truly forgiven person. Again this may sound strange, but for many for this to occur they need to speak these truths into their lives. Literally, they must forgive themselves with words that they speak out loud. This aspect is not typically a challenge for me, but if it was, later in the day after the incident with my son I would have later gone and literally said to myself—*I am forgiven for screaming at Micah*—and maybe even spoken these words more than once. As we all know, words are powerful. When we say them aloud, they can come to life. Again, in this case, it is important that the person speak in the first person and be specific about what they are forgiven for. On paper, this may seem unnecessary or silly, but this part of forgiving oneself and owning that truth is what some have trouble learning and accepting, and can keep their relationship with God at a stand-still.

A final important piece of someone genuinely living out the cycle of forgiveness is that they must relinquish that they can even change in the first place and that only Jesus can alter the way they act. On the one hand, we must make it priority to change our lives, but inevitably it is God who completes the work within us. To this day, I still struggle with anger and the incident I described happened almost fifteen years ago. I have changed, I have learned how to control my outbursts and I now understand that sometimes my anger can even be healthy, but there have also been times when I blew it even as just as two weeks ago! For some areas that we struggle, they may never be ended, and we will have to realize that we will in the future let ourselves and others down. Here is a truth—there will never be a day that I live on this earth in which I will be able to say that I am a perfect person. In our lives, there will always be areas that we struggle with even up until our last breath. With these struggles, we need to be diligent and continue to attempt to change these aspects of our lives, but at the same time, we need to relinquish this to God and allow him to complete this work in us. Even Paul late in his life shows us two important passages to meditate on—even he struggled in certain areas all the way up to his dying day:

> For I know that good itself does not dwell in me, that is, in my sinful nature. For I have the desire to do what is good, but I cannot carry it out. For I do not do the good I want to do, but the evil I do not want to do—this I keep on doing. (Romans 7:18-19)

> So I find this law at work: Although I want to do good, evil is right there with me. For in my inner being I delight in God's law; but I see another law at work in me, waging war against the law of my mind and making me a prisoner of the law of sin at work within me. What a

wretched man I am! Who will rescue me from this body that is subject to death? Thanks be to God, who delivers me through Jesus Christ our Lord! (Romans 7:21-25)

Again, a key ingredient in being Jesus' friend is living in the tension that I am a saint and that I am a sinner—we need to learn that it is okay that we are both people. No different than Paul did, it is a reality that we will have to learn to live with for the rest of our lives—we live in a fallen world and we are broken people trying to get better each day.

FACING THE PAST

Because this is what happens when you try to run from the past. It just doesn't catch up, it overtakes...blotting out the future.
Sarah Dessen

When the Japanese mend broken objects they aggrandize the damage by filling the cracks with gold, because they believe that when something's suffered damage and has a history it becomes more beautiful.
Barbara Bloom

Another area that a person must encounter if they wish to move to the point of friendship with Jesus is that they need to find the courage to seek healing in their lives. The major step forward in moving toward a friendship with God is looking at your past and facing your brokenness and wounds—wounds that you received from others and wounds that you have given yourself in the poor choices you have made. Too often in our lives we can put on masks and attempt to recreate ourselves for others. It is imperative that we live as who we really are and face the past and the problems in our personal lives. As I have said many times, we should never fake or hide the reality of our lives—Jesus wants to know us at the core of our being, the real person behind all of the facades we try to erect. Sometimes we put up those facades because of our past and history, and he demands that they come down.

Here is another truth—who we are today is often because of who we were yesterday. Our past and where we grew up and who are parents were and what happened to us in our early years inevitably influences us and often for a lifetime. While I don't fully agree with their findings, there are different research studies within psychology that have been done that seem to suggest that what happens to us prior to the age of five forever creates who we are. While these studies may over inflate their conclusions, there is at least an element of the truth to what they state—

we are very much a making of our past and upbringing.

A lot of people have some suspicions about looking at their past and for good reason. There have been pockets in psychology—Sigmund Freud, as an example—which have embellished and overstated different aspects of a person's upbringing and a parent's influence. However, without a doubt, how we were raised, how we were treated and nurtured, and if there was any abuse in our lives, be that physical, verbal, sexual, emotional or spiritual, can deeply influence are own mental, emotional or spiritual health. To not look at these dynamics and ramifications in our lives is short-sighted to say the least. Below are some basic questions to ask yourself in looking at how your past influences your life today.

- Who was the dominant parent in your family, your mother or your father? Was this parent nurturing or did you not have a close connection with this parent?
- Would you characterize your father as being a good parent? If you are man, did your father positively influence you to be masculine in a healthy way or did he condemn you in different ways verbally or non-verbally (e.g., *you're a wimp, you're worthless, you're such a girl*, etc.). If you are a woman, did your father positively influence you to be feminine or did he not nurture that side of you (e.g., he regularly told you were beautiful, he was appropriately affectionate with you, he tried to protect you in different ways, etc.). Now address these same questions about how your mother was as a parent.
- Here is an important question—how did your father or mother "image" God for you?
- In your teenage years and early adult years, were you able to speak openly with your parents, or were you shut down if you wanted to discuss a problem or issue in the family?
- With regards to your teenage years, how did your parents influence your sexuality? Were these open discussions or was the

topic never discussed?
- Were your parents too permissible (wanting to be your best friend) or too impermissible (very strict) in the rules that governed your life as a child and adolescent?
- Did you suffer any form of physical, spiritual, verbal or sexual abuse in your childhood?
- Did you witness physical, emotional or verbal abuse in your family?
- In your childhood, did you suffer any serious physical neglect?
- Did any of your primary caregivers (e.g., parents, grandparents or other family members) have mental health problems (e.g., substance abuse, bipolar disorder, borderline personality disorder, schizophrenia, serious depression, addictions, codependency, etc.)? Do you struggle with these same issues or similar ones?
- Were your parents ever separated or divorced? If so, when it occurred, how did this impact you?

When asking questions such as these, we need to honestly ask ourselves how these issues impacted us. We do know this, for those who have experienced a difficult or troubled childhood, it can have differing effects on their lives as children and when they become an adult. Some children and adults, when they experience loss or face maltreatment in some way can be more resilient than others. Likewise, from numerous studies, we also know that some adverse experiences in childhood are reparable and a person can move on with their life. In that same breath, some experiences can be toxic, meaning it can take years to deal with the pain of the serious damage that has occurred. As children, when we are party to any form of abuse, neglect or abandonment, we can lose track of the person we were meant to be—our real self that is trusting of others and especially toward God. Instead, to survive and cope in a family that is broken, for some of us, we go into hiding in some way, and we adapt to new surroundings and relationships in similar dysfunctional ways (e.g., emotionally distant, distrustful of others, codependence or people-pleasing, etc.). It can be common that from these experiences from many years ago that this can be the impetus for a myriad of problems that we face in our adult lives, and often it is easier to avoid them then to courageously acknowledge and face them.

WHERE OUR BROKENNESS COMES FROM

Typically, our brokenness and our sinful patterns originate in two different ways: 1) sin is engrained into our very nature because of the fallen state of our world; 2) we fall to different patterns of sin in response to the pain that we have never healed from or faced. It is in our best interest to face these past experiences to see how they might impact who we are and look at what we struggle with in regards to our personal problems and relationships. As someone said to me recently, she said that she was learning that "Your pain has to be taken to the same cross that your sins are." I think that says something very important to a lot of us.

A starting point in this journey of healing is beginning to share your story with someone. A lot of people think that the only person that they need to be open to is to God. That's a good place to start, but that's not the end all. In the book of James it says "Therefore, confess your sins to each other and pray for each other so that you may be healed." (5:16) In this verse, it's obvious that it is strongly suggesting that we need to seek out others who we can trust and share our faults and struggles with in our lives. But beyond this, I think what James was also stating is that it is imperative that we confess the sins that were done to us. What is the ending statement if we do this—we will find healing in our lives.

I remember in a small group I was in some years ago, I went with a bunch of guys up to a cottage in northern Michigan for a retreat in which the main purpose was so that we could come clean about the problem areas of our lives. It was a couple of days in which we just got away by ourselves and we could open up and share our dark secrets and some of our past. I remember a good friend telling us prior to us going that if the stuff we were going to share wasn't painful, it probably wasn't the stuff that we were supposed to share. Sharing our true souls in this way is almost always a difficult process. In a certain sense, it's like when we get sick—you have this awful thing inside that has to come out and the only way you are going to feel better is through a really messy and sometimes painful process. That is what accountability is in most cases—it's going to be uncomfortable and it's really not going to be something you jump to do. But that's okay, because if you do, in the end you will find deep healing, just as the book of James promises.

So with this type of sharing, with whom should you open up? This is the danger I have found some experience—they share their troubles and darkness with people they just should not trust. There are two dangers with this. First, you have the risk of sharing something deeply personal and the person you opened up to tells someone else all of the sacred stuff you've uncovered. They do not make what you shared confidential and carelessly share your secrets with others. Another danger is that the person you open up to is not a person of grace and after you have shared with them, their face shows a look of disgust and you walk away feeling dirty and terribly exposed. Without a doubt, these are not the ways in which you share your woundedness. We need to search out people we know and trust. They will be people who will be merciful with us because they are no different than you, and they have done things which they also deeply regret. They know that place well in which they are a wreck no different than you. A passage that comes to mind is when Jesus was offered to have dinner with a notorious prostitute. Many around him were astounded that he would accept such an invitation. He says this about her, "Therefore, I tell you, her many sins have been forgiven—as her great love has shown. But whoever has been forgiven little loves little." (Luke 7:47) I love that passage. Those who don't know their sins well, don't love very well either. However, in the reverse, we can also say, Those who have been forgiven much, love much. Seek out people in your life who have been forgiven much. Seek out those who know their brokenness well and at the same time, are also seeking their own healing. These are the safe people who you can pretty much share anything with them and they wouldn't even bat an eye.

Another thing that you can do is seek out professional help. I have never met a person who at some point in their life could not benefit from having a gifted counselor walk with them for a season. Too often people think that counseling is only for crazy people. Not at all. Counseling offers some advantages that some friendships just cannot provide. First, the conversations you have with a counselor or psychologist are guaranteed to be confidential. I cannot tell you how often in my practice that I have heard stories that a person had never shared in their life before simply because they knew I was bound to keep what I heard confidential. The security of knowing that what you share will never be revealed to anyone can give you the power to seek out help. Where in the past you perhaps have been afraid to open up about your story, now you can freely share everything about yourself because all that is said is going to be private.

Second, when you seek out a professional, you are being offered something that is invaluable and is sometimes hard to come by, and that is, you are receiving unbiased counsel. Too often, when our friends or family are offering us some advice or their opinion, it comes from a place of bias and partiality. Either they know us too well or they just do not have a good perspective on the situation, because what is often the case, they themselves are somehow involved in the issue that we are facing. For example, if you are having challenges in your marriage, your sister or best friend either wants to somehow stop the pain you are feeling or can't see how you are a part of the problem in your relationship. Sometimes our family and friends have a difficult time speaking a hard word or they want you to not suffer anymore and therefore, offer a quick solution. *Yep, HE is THE problem, isn't he?! Maybe you should just leave her—she was never good for you anyway.* A competent therapist can speak words of truth and challenge to you and they don't have to worry if you like them or not. After they refute your perceptions and your own biases, they don't have to go home with you and they can offer straight-forward advice.

Finally, counselors are trained and have experience in working with a myriad of problems. Good ones know what they are doing. Because counselors work with so many different situations and individuals, they garner an experience that overtime they learn what works for a given situation and what doesn't work. I know counselors who are great at working with marriages, others who know how to help someone with depression, and others still, who are expert at helping someone face a past trauma. Accomplished and trained counselors have a wealth of knowledge, and this can make the process of healing and growth happen more quickly because of their wisdom and experience. As a parallel, for years I tried to teach myself the game of golf and very slowly got better. A couple of years ago I sought out a golf teacher and professional. With just a couple of lessons, it was as if I improved overnight. He quickly saw what I was doing wrong and offered simple, but helpful suggestions in how I could improve my game. It's the same way when facing our personal struggles and problems—working with someone who knows what they are doing can make all the difference and sometimes healing and change can come rather quickly.

SOMETHING TO TRY

- Are there things you have never told anyone? Perhaps this was something that happened years ago or perhaps it's something that is on-going in your life at this time? What would it be like to be able to share these stories and events to someone and they would not tell a single soul? What would it be like to lift that burden off your shoulders?
- Are there areas of your life where you just can't seem to get "over

the hump?" Perhaps in your career you haven't gone anywhere and you can't figure out the root of the problem. Perhaps your marriage has never been really that satisfying since the second year. Perhaps you and your kid just can't seem to get along. What would it look like to get another person's perspective and see what they suggested?

I KNOW I SHOULDN'T

If you're feeling overwhelmed by all that you're doing, you are probably doing more than God has asked. Henry Blackaby

The difficulty of always feeling that you ought to be doing something is that you tend to undervalue the times when you're apparently doing nothing, and those are very important times. Brian Eno

Take these hands – teach them what to carry. U2

When you read the stories about Jesus sometimes you really see who he was as a person. In these glimpses, sometimes his personality shines through. He was intriguing to be around. He could openly be emotional. He carried with him dramatic and insightful stories. He was gently honest when he spoke to you. He was very deliberate about relationships. He was extremely bright. He had terrific compassion. He was very serious about his calling. He had great perspective about life.

And he was very conscious of his time and his limits. You've probably heard this one before, but one thing is certain, Jesus did not have a messiah complex. We read that at many different times you find him going to some remote place to be alone, to pray, to think, most likely to recharge his batteries (Matthew 14:23; Mark 1:35; Luke 5:16). Like any of us, Jesus also needed time to unwind, re-focus his energies and be by himself. When reading these stories, it seems like this was a common occurrence for him, not just some isolated event in his life. But an important point is that when he would remove himself from the throngs of people who would follow him, he inevitably was also disregarding their immediate needs to some degree. Essentially, he was saying *I will not care for you right now* and it seems like he was completely okay with that. I can picture him just as he was pulling on his cloak to make his way to be by himself, there would be some person there pleading for something more of him, "Jesus, just one more question?" Often, because of his celebrity, he would often in these instances have to firmly, but kindly tell them that it would have to wait for another time. You cannot be as popular as he was and not have the withal to let someone know that you weren't going to be able to help them in some way at that very moment.

If you think about it in these terms, it is remarkable to think of how many people Jesus didn't care for, heal or offer his wisdom and insight. Jesus was purposeful in how he served others. This is what we need to do as well. When we serve others, perhaps the most important question we should ask ourselves is—*should I be doing this?* Now granted, when someone asks for help in some way, in many of these cases, we should move into their lives and help them. But sometimes we maybe shouldn't. Perhaps we need to be more purposeful in how we help others.

God taught me this lesson shortly after I became a Christian. With this story, I also learned he has a great sense of humor. I was about twenty-one at the time and had taken the train into the city to meet a friend. Chicago was a bustle at that time because it was just a couple of weeks away from Christmas. Disappointingly, my friend had called and had to cancel our plans. Dejected, I began to walk the six blocks back to train in the December cold. About half way there, I heard someone yell out "Buddy, buddy!" I looked around and couldn't see anyone. After a second, I realized it was a man in a wheelchair who was hidden behind a car, and obviously homeless. As I approached him, he shouted with no regard for politeness, "Buddy, I need twenty bucks. Give me twenty bucks so I can go sleep and shower up at the Y. I need the money, man."

To say the least, I wasn't in the mood to be asked for money at that point—my friend had left me high and dry, it was cold, and because of that, I was frustrated and just not in the mood. My immediate response to him was that I didn't have twenty bucks. However, truthfully, I had one twenty dollar bill in my left jean pocket.

He again belted out, "Come on, man, I need a place to go!"

Again, without hesitation, I lied and said I had a friend who worked up at the McDonald's two blocks away and that I would get the money for him. Of course, I didn't have any friend who worked at McDonald's. I was frustrated, cold and trying to ditch this guy. I just wanted to go back home. Of course, he insisted I take him with him, and again, for whatever reason, I obliged. As I was pushing him up State Street in his wheel chair, he did something that to this day I still remember vividly. Loudly, with a multitude of people shuffling past us with their Christmas gifts in tow, he shouted, "Buddy, buddy! Pull over! Pull over!"

Confused, I pulled over to the side of the sidewalk near the curb, but before I reached it, I realized he had unzipped himself and was peeing on the sidewalk! Flush with embarrassment, the people passing by eyed us and obviously were wondering what we were doing. My first thought was, *Awesome, I am going to get arrested today*. After he zipped himself up, we continued on our way—I was pushing his wheel chair as quickly as I could so I could get this episode of my life over. As we reached the McDonald's, I rushed in the doors as he waited outside. I stood there, feeling entirely stupid and wondering what I was going to do. With him looking through the window, I acted like I was talking to one of the guys at the cash register. Finally, flustered and annoyed, I went outside to where he was, pulled out of my pocket the twenty dollar bill and shoved it into his hand. Then as quickly as I could, I made my way back to the subway station where I could head back home. As I got to the cashier window, I reached into my left jean pocket and as I rustled around to find my twenty dollar bill, and then realized I had given my new friend all of my money! I had absolutely no money to get home, and therefore, had to walk about three miles to a friend's apartment to get some money for my train ride home (remember, this is before the day of cell phones).

About three months after this incident, I was on the train heading back home from a class earlier in the day. As I was resting my eyes, I heard a loud voice exclaim, "Buddy, buddy! I need twenty buck so I can get a room at the Y." As I opened my eyes and adjusted them to the light, sitting right across from me was my friend who I had met that December day. Slurring his words badly and reeking of alcohol, at that moment, I realized my mistake three months earlier. That day, most likely, as I was walking those three miles in the Chicago cold to a friend's place to replace my twenty bucks, my "buddy" was not washing up at the Y and resting in a warm bed. Instead, he was huddle under Wacker Street with a whole bunch of vodka. This story has always reminded me that sometimes it can be okay to <u>not</u> help someone who is need.

LEARNING HOW TO SAY NO

And so therefore, this is the other lesson I learned—we can stop feeling like we have to do everything and help everyone at each instance. We should know how to say no when we need to say no. We should lose the power of the "should." I should do this. *I should call her back. I should go to church and help out. I really should go to that Bible study. I should be there for him. I probably should give them the money they asked for even though they have mismanaged their money for years.* This is what happened in my own life. There was a time when I had to do it all, I was going to save everyone who came in my midst. I would immediately answer each call. If you needed to see me immediately, I could accommodate. I was always immediately available. But it came at a cost. I was getting terribly worn down. I was not myself around our home. I was losing my relationship with my sons. And with this, I was slowly developing a messiah complex —it felt good to help someone and it was like a drug. I liked it so much that it was becoming my identity. It was becoming my idol. As always, God came to my rescue and said, D*ude, just stop!*

But to do this you have to humble yourself. Those who know how to say no are actually not callous or lazy, they simply know they cannot be there for the person at that point in time. They might even know that they don't even have the skills or gifts to help the person in the first place. Actually, in truth, there can be a humility in learning to say no to someone. I can't do it, also can mean I shouldn't do it. *Perhaps you need to do it yourself. Perhaps you need to speak to someone else. Perhaps you need to find help from someone else. Perhaps someone else needs to move into sacrifice and this will be their opportunity if I don't help you. If I do this thing you are asking of me, and I shouldn't, I am actually robbing you or someone else of the gift of helping you.*

Coupled with this, those who have found this freedom from the "should" are good at not having to be in the spotlight. Sometimes we can serve just because we want the applause or recognition and this is no reason to be serving God or anyone else. Often those who have to keep going in some way are doing it because they are serving because of the attention and for the limelight. Pride is the motivation, not a broken heart to help someone in need. Humility is not the incentive, but being seen is what excites some to keep on the go and serving in some capacity. They are motivated by the slap on the back or because of the prestige they receive.

The one who learns these things enjoys to serve when no one sees what they are doing. As Jesus challenged, their left hand does not know what their right hand is doing (Matthew 7:3). They are serving because someone is in need and they don't hope to get anything out of it—even a thank you is not needed. This person pays attention to Jesus' words that when they are doing something for someone else they are doing it for him (Matthew 10:42). This is so freeing when it comes to serving—I know that I don't' have to get anything out of the sacrifice, because in the end, in reality, I did it for the One who rescued me. That is reward enough.

When you learn how to not get caught in the "should," you also learn how to rest. This is what Jesus models for us in all of those different passages when he seeks to be by himself. "But Jesus often withdrew to lonely places and prayed." (Luke 5:16) It amazes me sometimes how bad I am at this. A lot of us always have to be on the go and for us to learn how to sit and listen to God is a challenge. This is an area Jesus is continuing to implore me to learn. Is this you as well? Those who know how to say no to others in some way are also good at finding solitary places, because when they are rested, they are able to handle the challenges that will eventually attempt to trip them up.

SOMETHING TO TRY

- Do you have a hard time saying no to people in your life? Your friends, your family, those at work, etc.? What can you learn from Jesus that you don't have to yes to everything? For those who struggle in this area, a great book to read on the topic is *Boundaries* by John Townsend and Henry Cloud.
- Do you do a good job at getting away by yourself, and I mean totally by yourself? Or are you the type of person (like me) who always has to have noise playing or you have to be doing something (e.g., the television, a book in hand, working on a project, the computer on your lap, talking to someone on the phone, etc.). Do you have a difficult time just sitting, praying, and listening for God's voice for your life? How often do you purposely put silence in your life to just try to listen to what God has to say to you?

LISTENING WITH BOTH EARS

God is like a person who clears his throat while hiding and gives himself away.

Meister Eckhardt

The heart is commonly reached, not through the reason, but through the imagination, by means of direct impressions, by the testimony of facts and events, by history, by description.

John Henry Newman

Devotion is not a passing emotion: it is a fixed, enduring habit of mind permeating the whole life and shaping every action...and it necessitates an abiding hold on Him, a perpetual habit of listening for His Voice within the heart, as of readiness to obey the dictates of that Voice.

Jean Grou

I didn't' learn how to pray until I was about twenty-seven years old. As I've mentioned before, this was about the time I was just beginning to learn how to be Jesus' friend. It was also at that time, he taught me how to not only talk to him, but also how to listen to what he had to say to me. Now granted, I "learned" how to pray probably when I was a toddler, but to understand prayer and how God uses it in a person's life—I didn't get this one until about the third decade of my life. When a person enters into a friendship with God, they begin (I emphasize the word *begin*) to learn how to talk to him and how to listen to him.

Prayer for a lot of people is just talking. However, when you have a conversation with a good friend over a cappuccino at a Starbucks, two things typically occur—you talk and you listen. This is typically how conversations occur. Ironically, for a lot of people, this isn't how prayer works for them. It often can be a one way street: they talk, but there isn't a whole lot of listening going on. It's as if God is just expected to be the good listener.

I am a huge fan of Walter Wangerin and love his writing. If you have never heard of him, you have to go get any of his books, because they are written with an eloquence and wisdom unlike any Christian author that I know. Wangerin is a prolific writer on a wide-range of subjects; he's written a novel that was awarded the National Book Award (essentially, the American novel of the year); books on marriage, prayer, adoption, the resurrection, inner-city ministry; he's even got a book of poetry. His latest book is about his journey having cancer.

One book he entitled *Whole Prayer*, which is simply a book which discusses how to pray. The book has a simple premise, but it is also very profound. Wangerin makes this proposition about prayer:

First, we speak,

While, second, God listens.

Third, God speaks,

While, fourth, we listen.

There is obviously a lot there in those four points, full of questions for us. How does one speak to God? Is there a formula or standard in how we should speak to God? What is the process in which God listens? How does God speak to us? And in what ways can we listen? One of the most important things I learned when I finished the book was this—isn't it amazing that God is always listening for us. Wangerin, in the book, makes this beautiful analogy of a sick child crying out for her mother and right away the mother comes into her room to take care of her. Almost as if even before the child cries out, the mother is there. As he writes, "And immediately with understanding came the active response of a mother whose love is nearly omniscient, whose heart is almost omnipresent."

This is no different than how God attends to you and me. Even before I know what I need, He does—that is his relationship to me as a Father—taking care of me. The Lord is moving ahead of me, trying to prepare the way so that I can pass through unharmed and unhindered. As my favorite Psalm declares:

> He brought me out into a spacious place; he rescued me because he delighted in me. Your right hand sustains me; you stoop down to make me great. You broaden the path beneath me, so that my ankles do not turn. (Psalm 18: 19, 35-36)

For our purposes, I would take Wangerin's wisdom one step farther: when one is praying there should be four essential things occurring: talking, listening, responding and then finally, expecting. Jesus offers us some important hints into what prayer looks like. Let's walk through a couple of these. In the fifteenth chapter of John, Jesus teaches two important and astounding things about prayer. The first is somewhat mysterious, but as his friend, he will make known to us everything that we need to know. That's an astonishing statement and it's important to take him at this word:

> I no longer call you servants, because a servant does not know his master's business. Instead, I have called you friends, for everything that I learned from my Father I have made known to you. (John 15:15)

What I hear in something like this is this—by deepening our relationship with God day by day, we can know and understand our lives and the world around us better. The Bible calls this kind of stuff wisdom. But in the verse above, Jesus adds this strange little phrase which foretells what prayer can also be about—"because a servant does not know his master's business." He seems to be inferring that if you are a friend of his, he will let you in on what his pursuits and intentions will be—again, for yourself and also for the world around you. So therefore, prayer on some level is the tool which God uses to draw us closer to not only him, but also to our very selves. We will learn who we are; who we are supposed to be and what we are supposed to do—today, tomorrow and twenty years from now. God through prayer will give us clarity in what our lives should look like. It's an amazing relationship to say the least.

WHEN WE DON'T TAKE NO FOR AN ANSWER

But beyond this, Jesus also shares with us another important element of prayer—it is so that he can provide for us. "If you remain in me and my words remain in you, ask whatever you wish, and it will be done for you." (John 15:7) Not that we will move to a health and wealth gospel, but it is right there in black and white and in plain English—God wants us to have what we wish and what we need. Now, will he always give us what we want? Absolutely not. But he will give us more than what most ask for. What I have found is that most people don't "ask" as Jesus commanded. They live meek and mildly and don't think they are deserving of what God truly wants to give them.

What might be some of the things that the Father might want to give us? How about:

- A restored life for a friend who has had a string of broken life-situations in their lives.
- Our material needs where we are not always living paycheck to paycheck and can actually have enough money to get the things we need, and some of the things we want.
- A thriving and intimate marriage that lasts beyond fifty decades.
- An inviting home where many enter its doors and find safety, joy and rest.
- Children who follow God in their own lives and have a future.
- The end of a temptation which has followed us for years.
- A long-lasting friendship in which we can be ourselves and share our joys and secrets.
- Even something as non-consequential as when you are looking for a parking spot in a busy downtown.

Let me light-heartedly explain that last one. Ever since I met Julie, I've always done something which she has always thought was weird, but at the same time, she has been amazed by. What is it? I often pray for parking spots. Some may find it disrespectful or flippant with my prayer life, but in almost every case, God answers my prayers evoking his words of "asking." Just two weeks ago we were in Washington D.C. and had to park downtown. Looking out at the streets, there was no way we were going to find a spot. It was a Saturday. It was 1pm and the busiest time of the day. And it was in the heart of where everything was. True to form, after looking for a spot for fifteen minutes, I simply asked, *Lord, we need a parking spot.* I kid you not, thirty seconds later as we neared our destination, right across the street from the National Gallery of Art sitting there was one open spot. It is true, God wishes to invade every aspect of our lives—even when it requires the need for having a spot to park your car in a crowded downtown!

At the end of day, God wants us to ask. As Robert Hamil wrote "God is not a power or principle or law, but he is a living, creating, communicating person—a mind who thinks, a heart who feels, a will who acts, whose best name is Father." No different than me as a father to my sons, I want to give them good things and this is how the Father relates to me. As another example of this from our family, I have another good illustration. When it comes to our two sons, they each have unique, but different personalities. As a case in point, one of my sons is always asking for stuff from me. *Hey dad, will you buy this _____ for me? Hey dad, can we go to the library? Hey dad, want to watch a movie with me?* Even when I am not in the mood to watch a movie, I usually consent and do what he asks. On the other hand, my other son rarely asks anything of me—he is very unselfish, almost to a fault. Even though I love both of my son's equally and dearly, my son who is always asking me for things, probably over the long run "gets" more from me than my other son, simply because he asks for more. Now granted, my other son is not left without any clothes on his back or doesn't get anything at all, but if he were to ask more from me, I would treat him no different than his brother. If it was good and appropriate, I would in most cases give him what he asks for.

If I apply this same concept to my life, this is how it works with our Father as well. Jesus made his teaching very clear, Those who ask, get. As Matt Redman wrote in one of his worship songs, "Nothing is too much to ask now that I have said I am yours." So God asks you at this moment, *What do you want from me?* And don't make it just one thing. Ask away and see what he does and what he gives. As the great missionary Hudson Taylor penned:

> The prayer power has never been tried to its full capacity.
> If we want to see mighty works of Divine power and grace wrought in the place of weakness, failure and disappointment, let us answer God's standing challenge, 'Call to me, and I will answer you, and show you great and mighty things, which you do not know.'

LEARNING HOW TO REALLY LISTEN

But obviously, prayer is not just about getting what we want, and in fact, this is not even high on the list of why prayer is so crucial to our lives. At the end of the day, prayer is about fostering and growing a relationship with God. As friends to him, we have the opportunity to come into a close relationship with the One who loves us deeply. This is the central purpose of prayer—to get to know him better. Through talking, listening, responding and expecting, our relationship with God will have the ability to grow to uncharted depths. Have you ever met someone you just really like a whole lot? Someone that when you are in their presence, it is easy and fun and engaging? A person who is kind, reassuring, and listens well to your stories and concerns you share? This is who your Father is. This is the reason for prayer; to get to know this Person at his deepest levels.

Because this is one of God's deepest drives, He wants to be known. He wants to speak. He wants to listen. And he wants to respond. If God has a desire, it is this—he deeply yearns for a relationship with us.

This is the chief reason why he created us like himself—to be in relationship. Now, does he need to be in this relationship? If we reject this want of his, will he saunter away angry, depressed and lonely? Will he cripple under the weight of being rejected? Of course not. God is completely secure in himself and does not need a relationship with us, but in his self-giving and self-sharing nature, he wants to give himself away to anyone who would want to share in what he has to offer.

But how does one pray? How does one have a conversation with God? Of course, asking something of him is easy and straight-forward. "God, I want _____." But again, to have a conversation means one has to listen. How does one listen to God? The main way in which we can listen to God is through the Scriptures he gave us. But even here, the Bible is conclusive in declaring that "The Word became flesh." (John 1:14) To listen to God on some level means that we need to engage him flesh and blood and hear the words he has to say to us personally. We want to genuinely hear his voice and while at this point in time, we cannot actually sit down and literally have a conversation with him, he still speaks. Somehow, someway, he does speak to us. Through the Holy Spirit, we can literally hear what he wants to share with us and he often does it in unique ways. In the Bible we have stories in which God spoke through a donkey, visions, an angel, even through a bush that had caught on fire. When desiring to speak with us, he will do anything to make sure that he gets his point across.

But how does one listen to God? Actually, listening to God is not complicated at all. In saying that, it does require some dedication and for you to section out time in your life to just sit and listen to him. There really isn't a formula, but some simple guidelines would be as follows:

1. Set aside about thirty minutes each time you pray. Make sure you find a quiet place where you won't be distracted. It sometimes can be good to find a favorite spot where you like to go (e.g., a favorite park, a comfy chair, outside on your deck, etc.)

2. To begin, take about ten minutes to read some Scripture. The Psalms or the Proverbs are a good place to start.
3. In terms of beginning to pray, ask for two things:
4. That the Lord would speak to you clearly.
5. That he would block out any voices from yourself or from any other demonic influence.
6. With a private journal that you use specially for this time of prayer, write down a question or two that would like to discuss with God. Now, wait and listen.
7. Without judging what you are writing, listen to your inner voice and begin writing down what you hear in your mind. You may be flooded with lots of words or just a few. Take about five to ten minutes to write what you are hearing the Holy Spirit say to you. During this time, some people like to use two pens of different color—with one, they use to write what their own thoughts are and with the other, what they believe God is saying to them.
8. In terms of deciding if what you heard was from God, here are some questions you should ask yourself:
    - Was what you wrote clear or just an impression of something? Sometimes what we write is for the present moment of our lives or for a later time when we piece together things from our lives. This is why keeping a prayer journal is important—it is so that you can go back and read it. Recently I was reading through one of my journals and I was astonished at something I had written four years ago as it clearly spoke into my life at that moment.
    - With what you wrote is it scriptural? Scripture is our authority and God does not contradict his Word. (Proverbs 30:5-6)
    - If it is an important decision that you must make, you

should always speak with other Christians about what you heard God saying. Do these friends confirm what you heard God say? (Proverbs 20:18, Proverbs 15:22)

This is a rudimentary framework for attempting to listen to God. If you would like to delve deeper, I highly suggest you read the classic by Leanne Payne entitled *Listening Prayer*. It will be worth your time. Remember, God is very inventive and creative in how he speaks to us and will use unique ways to create a conversation with us. Once you begin listening purposely to his voice, he will often speak to you in other ways, especially through others, through dreams, and who knows, perhaps even in a vision like he did with Peter! In your desire to get to know him, he will continue to make himself available to you and reveal many different things to you. Be on the watch, because again, he deeply desires to be your friend and hear from you and speak to you in evident and astonishing ways.

LIVING BY GRACE, THE TRUTH AND THE MYSTERIOUS

Twenty years from now you will be more disappointed by the things that you didn't do than by the ones you did do. So throw off the bowlines. Sail away from the safe harbor. Catch the trade winds in your sails. Explore. Dream. Discover.

Mark Twain

It is difficult to live in the present, ridiculous to live in the future, and impossible to live in the past. Nothing is as far away as one minute ago.

Jim Bishop

Language fits over experience like a straight jacket.

William Golding

When one becomes a friend of Jesus, there is great freedom, an interdependence with God to live our lives. Annie Dillard says it straight—she captures what being a friend of Jesus is all about—"It is life at its most free." Friendship with Jesus has this element in which there is freedom and where one can live life with maximum capacity. Alice Sebold has a phrase that also puts it in an eloquent way, "Where you can live at the edge of your skin as long as you wish." Jesus meant what he said when he told us that to be with him is of no burden (Matthew 11:30). Here, a person can continually become agile at living. This is the main purpose of learning how to be a friend to God—learning to live in his grace, his truth and through the mysteries that life offers us.

A way to look at this distinction is that when one begins to master a life of following Jesus, they know how to balance a life of *grace* and *truth* —first, for themselves and then for others. What do I mean by these two words? Grace is being able to look at your life and knowing that God *forgives*. On the other hand, truth is looking at your life and knowing that God holds you *responsible*. Jesus is our model and a verse flushes out this truth: "For the law was given through Moses; grace and truth came through Jesus Christ." (John 1:17) This is precisely how Jesus lived well. He was able to serve and move into another person's life in which he forgave them and was at ease with who they were, but he could also at the same time hold them responsible for their lives. He was easy to be around, but in the same moment, he could speak truth into your life, truth that you perhaps were not even aware of in the first place. In this respect, I think of a seemingly insignificant conversation he had with a woman he met on a random day.

> Now he had to go through Samaria. So he came to a town in Samaria called Sychar, near the plot of ground Jacob had given to his son Joseph. Jacob's well was there, and Jesus, tired as he was from the journey, sat down by the well. It was about noon. When a Samaritan woman came to draw water, Jesus said to her, "Will you give me a drink?" (His disciples had gone into the town to buy food.)
>
> The Samaritan woman said to him, "You are a Jew and I am a Samaritan woman. How can you ask me for a drink?" (For Jews do not associate with Samaritans.
>
> Jesus answered her, "If you knew the gift of God and who it is that asks you for a drink, you would have asked him and he would have given you living water."
>
> "Sir," the woman said, "you have nothing to draw with and the well is deep. Where can you get this living water? Are you greater than our father Jacob, who gave us the

well and drank from it himself, as did also his sons and his livestock?"

Jesus answered, "Everyone who drinks this water will be thirsty again, but whoever drinks the water I give them will never thirst. Indeed, the water I give them will become in them a spring of water welling up to eternal life."

The woman said to him, "Sir, give me this water so that I won't get thirsty and have to keep coming here to draw water."

He told her, "Go, call your husband and come back."

"I have no husband," she replied.

Jesus said to her, "You are right when you say you have no husband. The fact is, you have had five husbands, and the man you now have is not your husband. What you have just said is quite true."

"Sir," the woman said, "I can see that you are a prophet. Our ancestors worshiped on this mountain, but you Jews claim that the place where we must worship is in Jerusalem."

"Woman," Jesus replied, "believe me, a time is coming when you will worship the Father neither on this mountain nor in Jerusalem. You Samaritans worship what you do not know; we worship what we do know, for salvation is from the Jews. Yet a time is coming and has now come when the true worshipers will worship the Father in the Spirit and in truth, for they are the kind of worshipers the Father seeks. God is spirit, and his worshipers must worship in the Spirit and in truth."

The woman said, "I know that Messiah" (called Christ) "is coming. When he comes, he will explain everything to us."

Then Jesus declared, "I, the one speaking to you—I am he."

I love this exchange on so many levels. First, Jesus shows us how to be graceful—no normal Jewish person would be talking to a Samaritan—they were the outcasts of their day. Imagine the most disgraceful person you could imagine, this is this woman. Not many would be caught dead talking with her. Jesus right away shows tremendous grace by simply exchanging words with her. It is a beautiful truth, Jesus would talk with anyone no matter who they were or where they had been. Beyond this, Jesus knows who he is dealing with and it is a woman who has not lived a life most would respect—she has been married five times and is now living with another man. You can do the math on this one and know how most people would respond to a woman such as this. She is a woman of "ill-repute," and yet Jesus doesn't even blink an eye.

And then the conversation gets interesting. It goes way beyond just who she is and what she represents. She shows her true colors and basically Jesus is dealing with the worst used car salesman ever. Essentially, this Samaritan woman is just jabbering and talking nonsense. She is trying to twist the conversation to try to hide who she is. Just as with any of us, Jesus catches on quickly and directs the conversation in a way that he wants. He turns the conversation and it is he who asks the questions of her. As T.S. Eliot so powerfully poses in one of his poems about Jesus: "Oh my soul, be prepared for the coming of the Stranger. Be prepared for him who knows how to ask questions." This is Jesus, the one who knows how to ask penetrating questions of you, me and of this Samaritan woman. He won't be talked into a lemon that is going to break down ten minutes after he drives it off the lot. He is going to bring truth to her life, and he is not going to be snowed by her words or the provocative dress she is wearing. I love what he interjects; he poses a simple request of her. "He told her, 'Go, call your husband and come back.'"

He knows full well what her answer would be if she answered him honestly. She has no husband and he is about to get at the heart of the question about the life she has lived. Again, she tries to divert his question and schmooze him by getting at any male ego, "You are a prophet." Essentially, she is trying to butter him up—*You are so special, important and influential.* But Jesus ignores her compliment and again in startling directness, basically tells her she is doing it all wrong. "You Samaritans worship what you do not know....Yet a time is coming and has now come when the true worshipers will worship the Father in the Spirit and in truth." Truth hurts, but Jesus speaks it when necessary and now is the time. He will not be seduced by a woman who is attempting to escape his deepest questions. The dialogue then ends in a way that only he could. Again, she tries to change the conversation: "I know that Messiah is coming."

Beautifully and directly, Jesus simply offers here these words, "Then he declared, 'I, the one speaking to you—I am he.'" Can it get more truthful and honest than this? Only once before did Jesus share with someone who he truly was in this respect to being the Christ, the Savior of the world. In this abrupt and seemingly insignificant conversation with a wanton woman, he tells it like it is. Grace and truth, all in one conversation.

Those stuck in the believer and servant stages of faith waver toward one corner or the other with these two aspects of grace and truth. They have a difficult time holding these characteristics in tension, first for themselves and then for others. On the one hand, believers see God as always graceful and that he always forgives no matter what they do. As mentioned in previous chapters, they do not feel like they have to be responsible for their actions, no matter how heinous. Therefore, if one is too easy on themselves, they obviously will be too easy with others and a whole slew of problems will go overlooked. In the reverse, those who are stuck in the servant stage of faith, only sense God's truth and they are forever responsible and never truly forgiven. Because this truth is usually at the forefront of their mind, they are always missing the mark and always living without forgiveness. Again, once they put this burden on themselves, as we discussed at length in the previous section, they will inevitably put this tremendous weight on others.

Friends of Jesus put the weight of grace and truth on their lives in equal respects—first, on themselves and then onto others. On the one hand, they are at ease with themselves and on the other; they know when they have to make changes in their lives because of sin patterns or personal problems. They are also adept at doing this with others, no different than Jesus did with the Samaritan woman. They are at ease in being relationship with someone who doesn't have it altogether and at ease to challenge the waywardness of someone's life. Of course, being able to live in these two tensions can be challenging, but those who wish to live as Jesus did, must learn how to be graceful and truthful.

LOOKING THROUGH A GLASS DARKLY

But beyond learning how live in grace and truth, the other thing that some Christians have a really hard time doing is living with the grace of mystery. I remember one time my son and I were discussing dinosaurs to which he was speaking about some aspect of the issue very definitively.

He demanded: "Dad, I've spent lots of time thinking about this and I think I've nailed it. I know I'm right!" As the infamous 13th Chapter of I Corinthians maintains, "For now we see through a glass, darkly; but then face to face: now I know in part; but then shall I know even as also I am known." Those who have entered into a friendship with Jesus can live in the tension of looking through that darkened glass.

One can learn how to live a life where we don't have all the answers. A friend's two year old drowns in their backyard pool—you don't have to say a word. Silence is golden in times like these and when your friend asks that inevitable question, "Why did God allow this to happen?!" It is okay to just listen and sit with them in their pain. With some things that we experience in life, there are not always hard and fast answers. When a friend who is a remarkable and giving person, loses not one or two, but now three children to miscarriages, when she asks that same question, "Why does God allow this happen to me—doesn't he understand how much I desperately want to be a mother and have a child of my own?!"—again, in these times, we see through a glass darkly.

In my own life, I have had to second-hand face these same types of questions. Julie's parents were killed when she was just five years old. From what I've been told they were a wonderful couple—her dad a principal of a Christian school and her mom a devoted nurse and mother. But on a Friday evening while driving home to Michigan, a car veered into their lane and they were hit head on by an oncoming truck. Instantly, they were killed as Julie and her sister were left unharmed in the back seat. Instantly, life was dramatically changed forever for her as her mom and dad would no longer be able to be there for her. Some years ago, I was listening to a song and when I heard the lyrics I instantly thought of Julie and her loss.

> I always knew you
> In your mothers arms

I have called your name

And when you write a poem
I know the words
I know the sounds
Before you write it down
When you wear your clothes
I wear them too
I wear your shoes
And your jacket too

I always knew you
In your mothers arms

Rest in my arms
Sleep in my bed
There is a design
To what I did and said

Vito's Ordination Song, Sufjan Stevens

When I listened to those words, "I always knew you in your mother's arms" that was an image that Julie on many occasions painted for me of her own mother. We inherited from her grandmother the rocking chair that Julie and her mother would sit in when she was a little girl and this is the prominent memory she has of her mom. As the song ended the first time I heard it, the words haunted me as Sufjan Stevens uttered, "There is a design to what I did and said." In an experience like Julie has lived out in losing a mother and father who loved her dearly, what was the purpose of them being killed on that Indiana highway? While there is a comfort in God saying to her that she can "rest in his arms;" there are still multitudes of questions that go unanswered. Julie, like you and I, live our lives by looking through a glass darkly.

Again, we don't have to have all the answers to life's questions. Life is complex, beyond our imagination and while God has a tremendous plan for our lives, each of us in some way or another will face tragedies and loss in some way. In doing so, we will face all kinds of questions that for now just do not have answers. As Albert Einstein said, "The fairest thing we can experience is the mysterious." Now that I am in my fourth decade, I have learned that life can sometimes be cruel and difficult at times. I have faced many challenges, in which I have cried out, God—why?! Why is there such extreme poverty? Why do children have to be hurt in some form or another? Why do people do such awful things? Why does my friend's marriage have to fail? Why did that tornado have to sweep through that town and wipe everything and everyone out? Why is there disease and death? Why do I have to die? Why?!

A book like *The Problem of Pain* by C.S. Lewis can be helpful in trying to understand life's complexities and challenges. I remember reading his infamous words that "God whispers to us in our pleasures, speaks in our conscience, but shouts in our pains: it is His megaphone to rouse a deaf world." And this brought some form of answer, but not until I continued on and heard his words, "God will look to every soul like its first love because He is its first love."—this was the real answer I sought. I am his first love and no matter what I face that will not change, and that will not alter his plan for my life and the life of my family—no matter what we have to face—good or bad.

SOME QUESTIONS TO PONDER

- Usually, when living in the two tensions of grace and truth, we lean toward one characteristic over the other. Are you typically more graceful or more truthful?
- What do you need to do to change to grow in these areas, either becoming more graceful or truthful with your life? In looking at

Jesus' exchange with the Samaritan woman we see some important aspects to living by grace and truth. Some of them are:

- Engaging with someone we might not normally be comfortable being in relationship with.
- Being at ease and adept in having conversations that might be difficult to talk about.
- Being able to enter into a conversation in which there might be disagreement or conflict.
- Learning how to steer a conversation in a way which is most helpful for you and the other person.
- Using Jesus as our example, learning how to ask good questions of others.
- Learning skills or being open to the Holy Spirit so that we are not deceived or being manipulated by others.
- Having the insight to share some important biblical truth with someone.

- Looking at the list above, are there any areas you need to grow? If so, specifically what relationships are in your life that you need to learn from Jesus in being graceful and truthful?
- An important area of our lives that some of us need to grow is learning how to live in the place of mystery—the place where we don't have to have all the answers. In what areas of your life, do you need to do this and learn to be okay with "looking through the glass darkly?" How in your life can you become a better listener to God and to others and not always have to have the final word? How can you "let God be God" and simply rest in that assurance?

GETTING TO KNOW YOUR PAPA

And when you appear all the rivers sound in my body, bells shake the sky, and a hymn fills the world.

Pablo Neruda

We do not believe in ourselves until someone reveals that deep inside us something is valuable, worth listening to, worthy of our trust, sacred to our touch. Once we believe in ourselves we can risk curiosity, wonder, spontaneous delight or any experience that reveals the human spirit.

e.e. cummings

God loves each of us as if there were only one of us.

Saint Augustine

Essentially, I grew up a latch-key kid in the late 1970's and early 1980's. A lot of my friends did as well. This generation was really one of the first generations in which a lot of kids my age were raising themselves and we were left to our own devices. Often both parents worked and for a lot of kids my age, there just wasn't a lot of "adult-supervision." With this, in my teen years, my parents were really not role models for me, my friends were. However, in all this, I desperately wanted a father who knew me and cared for me in tangible ways. Even those who grow up in the best of families can feel this way, but for some reason I felt it especially deeply.

There was for me a marking experience at this point in my life which looking back really has shaped who I am as a person. Like a lot of freshman in high school, that school year was hell. Beyond a shadow of a doubt, it was the worst year of my life. Something happened to me and I was at the pinnacle of lostness and depression. My friendships dried up and I was diving deep into despair. I'm not sure how all this came about, but I was in a very bad place. Suicide was at the forefront of my mind and it seemed like the most reasonable answer.

I can recall vividly that night that I decided to end it all. I was very upset: crying, angry, deeply sad and alone. At that point in the life of my family, my dad worked second shift and my mom had a ceramics business which she ran out of our garage. That night she was working with the other women out there when I was plotting my demise. I was going to poison myself. I took some rat poison from under the sink and shoveled it out onto some vanilla ice cream. As it poured out, my tears began to well larger and deep inside I wanted nothing of what I was plotting. But as with many who face taking their own lives, it seemed like the best answer at that moment. After a minute of reflection, I knew I couldn't eat that concoction and so I emptied it down the disposal. At that point, I knew I was in a very bad place and so I decided to reach out to my mom for help. I walked toward our remodeled garage and mumbled to her from behind the screen door, "Mom, I need to talk to you."

"Kelly, I can't talk to you right now. I am working," or something similar was her response. I turned from the door, tears sliding down my face. I knew what I needed to do and I ventured into my mom and dad's bathroom and emptied what I thought to be a bottle of aspirin into my mouth and went to bed.

Near four a.m., I woke up sicker than a dog. I began throwing up and I was very out of it. Even though I had never experienced these sensations, later I would learn that it was similar to being drunk. I was bewildered. I was numb. I was confused. However, two incredible things happened at that moment. While laying in bed and looking up at the ceiling, I decided I really wanted to live. I didn't want to die in the least and I vowed I would never go down this road again. Life was for me, no matter how bad it got.

But another odd thing happened. At that moment, internally I realized I was putting to much weight on counting on others. This notion may seem odd, but it became one of the clearer realities that I would learn. That night I needed someone more than ever and no one was to be found (or so I thought). At that time, in a lot of ways, my mom was the center of my life. I counted on her. For the most part, she seemed like she was always there; always being able to be counted on. In this vivid experience, I realized that simply was not how life always works. No one could be that person for me—I was expecting too much to which only God could provide. I could not always count on her or anyone else—at least in the ways I wanted. There was only one Person I could genuinely count on—the One who always comes through in the clutch when I need him. Strangely, through trying to take my life, I learned a lesson that has stuck with me—only God is reliable and constant. When we expect others to be that type of person for us, it always goes wrong.

Some years later, about four to be exact, this moment in time came together into clarity for me. As I spoke about earlier in the book, it was when I very slowly began to trust that God was real and that he was there for me. I was learning a new thing. While my mom and dad were doing the best they could, God was slowly going to teach me that I should only become dependent upon him. At this point, in my life, I never realized that or knew that. I had put too much hope and weight on others to make me satisfied, fulfilled and happy. Again, only God could do that. This was the first step in me realizing I really did have a Father who cared for and protected me. For the first time, I was beginning to understand that I was God's treasured son, his heir and child.

ACTING LIKE AN ADULT WITH GOD

What is like to be God's child? At different points in the Scriptures, God tells us that he wants us to know him as Papa. At many different points, Jesus refers to God as "Abba," which in our vernacular is the word we use for "papa." It is a beautiful word, especially when one associates it with God. There maybe isn't a better word in the English language one could use to create a picture of who he wants to be in our lives. When I think of a papa, I think of a generous father who is always looking after his children. I think of a father who is easy to be with and one with whom you can share anything. I think of a father who you can ride on his big shoulders as you swim in the ocean. I think of a father who instructs and guides you with a smile. This is one of the final steps in becoming God's friend—to get to know him as a Papa, as a Father unlike any you have ever met.

When one goes to this place in their life, things change and life is transformed. It's when you become okay in your own skin; humbly, you know that you are special; you look in the mirror and see a highly valued person. The Scriptures validate and insist that we are unique, sacred and tremendous creations made by his own hand and made in his image—made like him in so many ways. You've read it before, you've heard it before, you are special, you are a child of God. You were made with a great purpose and able to do great and tremendous things. You are a treasured person not just because God loves you as his first love, but also because who he made you to be—even with all of your oddities and intricacies. This truth makes me think of a quote that Thomas Lynch made about "growing up"—there is a parallel in learning to grow up and become Jesus' friend.

> There is about midlife a kind of balance, equilibrium--neither pushed by youth nor shoved by age: we float, momentarily released from the gravity of time. We see our history and future clearly. We sleep well, dream in all tenses, wake ready and able.

God is highly relational and he wants to be in a Father-son/Father-daughter relationship with you. In this sense, I like how C.S. Lewis wrote about God's personality and nature. He saw that God, who is triune in nature, as someone who is "super-personal." We can't even imagine such a person. I like that phrase Lewis uses—"super-personal"—God is personal to an extreme. Actually, he is more than a person. Think about that one for awhile. I believe there can be a comfort and an excitement that one can find in such an understanding. One day we will all stand face-to-face to this ultimately personal Person. Better yet, we can know this super-personal Person even today. This is his main joy and pursuit he wants for our lives—for us to truly know him for who he is.

But to truly to get to know your Papa, what I have learned in walking this path with many in my practice as a counselor, my work as a pastor, and in my own life, is that your relationship to him needs to change in a unique and specific way. Let me describe what I mean by this. Within psychology, there is a theory called Transactional Analysis and it attempts to explain how we can experience relationships in a mature way. The psychologist Eric Berne in the 1960's created this theory in which he hypothesized that we use "roles" in adulthood with the different types of relationships we have, be that with our parents, our spouse, our kids, our boss—with anyone who is in our life. The theory uses the analogy of the relationship between a parent and the child. Typically, according to Transactional Analysis, there are three different personalities or roles (Berne called them ego-states) that we use throughout life in the relationships we have:

- *The Parent:* the role in which you will mimic how a typical parental figure behaves (e.g., instructing, talking down to the other person, always trying to control the situation, disciplining for bad behaviors, dominating the relationship, etc.)
- *The Child:* the role in which you will regress to a place in which you behave and feel as a typical child might (e.g., allowing yourself to be talked down to, often being fearful or feeling inadequate around another person, letting yourself be controlled by the other person, rarely voicing your real opinion to the other person, etc.)
- *The Adult:* the role in which you are "yourself"—you offer your own opinion freely; you are able to enter into conflict and disagree with the other person; you are authentic in how you are

around the person; you are confident in yourself in all circumstances.

To try to make sense of all of that is above, the premise simply refers to how we act in the relationships around us—whether it is with your spouse or someone you work with—do you act like a parent, a child or do you act in a healthy way, like an adult. A real-life example of this is when I met with an attorney as a client a while back. He was a well-known defense attorney who was highly sought after and accomplished in his work. However, one of the issues that came out in counseling is that if he was ever around his dad, he would inevitably act like the thirteen year old boy he used to be. In part, his father dominated him, but in the same degree, he would also allow the relationship to continue in this unhealthy way. When he was with his dad, he would always play the part of a child who always needs help or was never quite sure of himself. Whenever he was around his dad, he was always walking on eggshells, never said what he really wanted to say, and could never really be himself. For him, his father was not a friend, and primarily that was because they didn't have a real relationship where they could talk to one another about anything as adults. His dad had remained the *parent* and he continued to act like a *child*.

As a counselor, we encourage clients caught in these relationships to use the premise of Transactional Analysis and to act like an adult when confronted with these types of relationships and situations. We literally ask them to change the role they are playing in the relationship. In this case, when this client spent time with his dad, he needed to stay in the character of the lawyer who he was Monday to Friday and not the apprehensive teenage boy he was so many years earlier. Around his father, he needed to be sure of himself and speak what was really on his mind. Simply put, he needed to act like an adult when he was around his dad. Often, it can be the mere recognition of the role the person is playing (i.e., in this case, this man was staying in the role of the child) that people can begin to act differently in these relationships. Oftentimes, when one begins to act the part, the change can become permanent. There is no need to explore one's past; no need for medications; no need of lengthy counseling. Relationships in our lives begin to change because we begin to change. It's what the Bible classifies as repentance or to change one's thinking and move in a different direction in your life. In the situation with this attorney, just after a couple of months, when he acted like himself around his father, his dad also responded in a healthy way and today they have a relationship that is growing closer. With this little change, this man and his father have a maturing friendship in which now they both can now be themselves.

This area is also one of the major catalysts in which our relationship with God can expand. When it applies to Transactional Analysis, for us to deepen our relationship with God we need to stop acting like a child around him. For some of us, we literally need to change our relationship with God and learn how to be ourselves around him. Yes, we are children of God, but we can also have an adult relationship to him. God wants us to be authentic with him, and to have a relationship in which we can say anything to him. Let me give you another parallel. Right now both of my sons are in high school and a significant way that I relate to them is as a parent. Often, I tell them what to do; I control when they are to be home; I guide them if they stray. However, in just a few years, both of them will be adults and starting a new life on their own. When that occurs, how I relate to them will have to change. I will have to move out of the role of the parent and they will have to stop acting like children. Mutual trust will become a part of the relationship. They will take responsibility for their lives and begin to truly act like adults. A friendship will emerge between my sons and I, and our relationship will mature and expand. This is precisely what God wishes for us as our relationship with him as it grows and expands.

As the infamous 13th chapter of Corinthians states: "When I was a child, I talked like a child, I thought like a child, I reasoned like a child. But when I became an adult, I set aside childish ways." (1 Corinthians 13:11) When I'm counseling the people that I work with—this is where I press them to go with their relationship with God—to act like an adult with him. By far, it is the most important mark of faith. It is more important than the day you were wed; more important than the day when your children were born; even more important than that day you decided to believe in God for the first time. It is truly the day that you really wake up and understand not only who God is, but just as importantly, who you are. You truly begin to relate to him like never before. You become his friend. This is the beauty of how this relationship grows, not only do I change in my relationship to him, but now God changes in how he relates to me. As I become more sure of the relationship, as I learn how to have a voice in the relationship (one here can think of Abraham's relationship to God that we find in Genesis 18), God unveils who he is in remarkable ways. As the 16th century saint, Teresa of Ávila penned, "The feeling remains that God is on the journey too." That is the truth, God wants to journey with us as we deepen our relationship together—he desires to be Friend, Lord and Papa—all in the same breath.

Epilogue

Learning to Walk on Water

EPILOGUE:
LEARNING TO WALK ON WATER

The Lord would speak to Moses face to face, as a man speaks with his friend.
Exodus 33:11
I want to be like water. I want to slip through fingers, but hold up a ship.
Michelle Williams

I have a picture in my office at home that might be the one thing that I own that I treasure the most. It is a picture taken in 1972 of me and my grandfather. He and I are sitting snuggled tight in his favorite chair. He is wearing a plaid, blue and white checkered short-sleeve shirt; he has on his Saturday khakis that he would wear while working in his enormous garden; and he is sporting some glasses that kids today would say are hipster and cool. I am wearing some blue shorts, an orange shirt, and the biggest smile a five year old could have. Why is this picture so important to me? It is the perfect image of who Jesus is to me today — me sitting in his lap.

My grandfather was easily the most important person to me when I was growing up. I could argue that there has not been a deeper influence on me in all of my life. Let me share a little back ground. The year that picture was taken is when my biological dad left my mom and I. One day, he just picked up and left and never turned back. I don't really have any memories of my dad in those years and it wasn't until I was nineteen that I went and searched him out and finally met him. At that moment in time, when I was just five years old, it seemed as if I was left fatherless. How untrue that really was.

When my dad packed his bags and left, it left my mom in a serious bind—she was now a single mom, she only had a part-time job and a mortgage to pay. We were always close to my grandparents and so the most sensible thing to do was to move in with them. We moved just a couple of miles away and for two years we lived with my grandparents in their small two bedroom home with its one bathroom. I think at best its size would be about 750 square feet—in today's standards, it would be considered a small apartment. For the entirety of their fifty-five year marriage, my grandparents lived and died there. Though it was small, it was the perfect home.

As you can imagine, with this sort of background, my grandparents had a humble and simple life. To this day, I am so grateful for that heritage. My grandfather worked for over forty years at the local Roper plant making refrigerators and stoves. My grandmother worked as well—second-shift at a factory that she also gave forty years of her life. I have vivid memories in that fifth year of mine, when my mom and I lived with my Grandma and Grandpa Stutz. Every week night my grandfather and I at ten o'clock at night would drive and pick up my grandmother from work, because she never learned how to drive. When we would awake the next morning, I can remember an early breakfast being made by my grandmother's hand—always an egg, two strips of bacon, a piece of toast and some sweet orange juice from the carton. And most importantly, I remember my grandfather, a solid place to stand in a time of confusion and tumult.

My grandfather was a simple, but an extraordinary man. He served on the board of his church for many years. He was an extremely devoted family man, where even to this day, not just I, but most of my cousins would also tell you that he was one of the most important persons also in their lives. And he had two vices—he loved the Chicago Cubs and he enjoyed wearing nice clothes. My grandfather was the sharpest dressed man at his church, and you would have never guessed that during the work week he was getting his hands greasy and grimy working under a factory roof. He bought some of the finest suits, fedoras and ties, and he taught me early on that "it's the clothes that make the man." And he loved the Cubs—a "gift" he gave to me which to this day I will never forgive him because they are always losing. On many occasions, I remember driving up to Wrigley Field, both just he and I, or with some senior group, and we would sit in Wrigley Field and watch the Cubs lose another baseball game. Here is a fitting antidote—I think in all of the games I personally went to—the Cubs won only one game...

As I have alluded to, my grandfather was one of the hardest working people I have ever known, but beyond that, he was a good man. I never heard him say an unkind word about anyone. He was always honest, even to the point that on one occasion I remember him returning to the bank teller because she gave him an extra five dollar bill. He was an ever-faithful and loving husband. That was what my grandfather was to me—he was solid, like a branch of a tree that you could hang onto and know it would never break. Everyone should have a person like my grandfather in their life, because for me, in a way, he is a picture of what God must be like—generous, kind, caring, wise, faithful, sacrificing, humble—I could go on and on.

PUTTING IT ALL TOGETHER

Jesus can be this person for us and we can have someone even more solid than what my grandfather was for me. When Jesus spoke about himself, he clearly emphasized that he desires a deep relationship with us, even to the point of calling it friendship (John 15:15). He wants to be a safe, secure place for us where we can learn more and more about him and where we can learn just as much about ourselves. In our relationship with God, we can ease our lives into His and become who we were meant to be. This is what he told us it would be like. We will look into his face, friend to friend, and it would be as natural as anything we have ever experienced.

But for any of this to begin, we need to seriously look at our lives. Are you caught in that believer stage of faith? Is God distant from you because it is you that has moved away from him? Could you care less about how you live life and you truly think that the choices that you make don't matter? Have you grown up in the church, but never made a genuine commitment to God, making the claim that you were going to live for him and him only? Perhaps you are the type of person who at the end of the day, you live your life as if you don't need God. Is that you—are you so self-sufficient that God is a nuisance in how you want to live? But with all of this, you also know that your life is not on track and that just around the corner a crisis of some kind could overtake you. Are you in a place in your life that when you look at yourself in the mirror, you realize that your whole life needs a significant overhaul?

For others, perhaps you grew up in the church, but this thing about friendship with God is entirely foreign to you. Does everything have to be perfect and in its right place in your life, but in living this way, you never seem to add up to this standard? Have you when you look back over the years, you have served in many different ways, but almost always out of obligation and not because you really wanted to? And there is something else—deep down, something is missing, and also something is hidden in you that is dark and secret. Instead of being in friendship with God, you really have become just a religious person. Yes, you can speak eloquently about grace or forgiveness, but to know this deep down in your soul, you've never really experienced that (and somehow, someway you would really like to). Perhaps a common theme for your life is control—to control your relationships, your marriage, your kids, even your relationship with God. If this is you, Jesus is waiting for you—grab his hand and learn how to become his friend.

There are many shapes and sizes to being a Christian. But with this, we need to make our days count and attempt to develop our relationship with the One who created us. The choice is ours—whether it is living indifferently or ungraciously toward the seriousness of our lives. Life is short and we need to make the most of it, especially as it relates to becoming a friend to God. In our kitchen for about sixteen years has hung a picture that quotes a Psalm: it says this:

> Teach us to number our days, that we may apply our hearts to wisdom. (90:12)

We need to count our days and the wisest thing we can ever do is move into a friendship with Jesus. For the person who keeps God at a distance in whatever way they do, they miss out on so much. Remember, he wants all of our lives, not just the edges or the crumbs of our lives. Some years ago, I came across the beautiful epitaph that the poet Gregory Corso wrote for himself. It lies etched on his gravestone in Rome. It simply reads:

> Spirit
>
> is Life
>
> It flows thru
>
> the death of me
>
> endlessly
>
> like a river
>
> unafraid
>
> of becoming
>
> the sea

On some level, we are all afraid to come to God. No different than Adam and Eve after they had wronged the One who had created them, each of us looks for all kinds of ways to run and hide. But in every situation in our lives, he is right there trying to find where we are hiding. For each and every person, no matter where they are, where they come from or what kind of lives they lead, he is waiting for each of us to courageously pursue him. Each and every day, he is speaking to us in a singular way. Just as he wishes to be sought after, he will pursue us in creative ways—we just need to have our eyes open to his coming. Just like that river in Corso's epitaph, we have to decide to be unafraid of moving into the sea. To be unafraid of the most daunting thing we will ever do—to learn how to be friends with God. When we do this, when we make that decision—we will then be able to swim out to him into the waves that at first we thought would overtake us. But here was the reality of the situation—we didn't need to swim at all. We could actually walk on the waves, because he already had shown us how. In the end, we learned how to take his hand, and we learned how to look him squarely in the face gaining a confidence we never had before. We were unafraid of what might happen when we took that first step—we were unafraid of the waters that now we could walk on with ease.

THE END

ABOUT THE AUTHOR

Dr. Kelly Bonewell is an author, counselor and speaker. He is the Director of Congregational Care at [Ada Bible Church](). He has over 20 years of counseling experience which has focussed on spiritual problems, sexuality, and other emotional/psychological issues. Kelly lives in Grand Rapids with his wife, Julie and their two sons.

For more information, please see his website at www.kellybonewell.com.